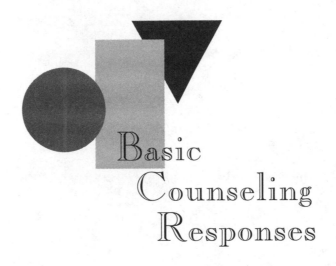

Basic
Counseling
Responses

Basic
Counseling
Responses

A Multimedia Learning System
for the Helping Professions

Hutch Haney
Seattle University

Jacqueline Leibsohn
Seattle University

Brooks/Cole • Wadsworth

I(T)P® An International Thomson Publishing Company

Belmont • Albany • Bonn • Boston • Cincinnati • Detroit • Johannesburg • London • Madrid • Melbourne
Mexico City • New York • Pacific Grove • Paris • Scottsdale • Singapore • Tokyo • Toronto • Washington

Acquisitions Editor: *Lisa I. Gebo*
Marketing Manager: *Liz Gilley Poulsen*
Editorial Assistant: *Susan Wilson*
Production Editor: *Nancy L. Shammas*
Production Service: *Anne Draus, Scratchgravel Publishing Services*

Permissions Editor: *May Clark*
Manuscript Editor: *Kay Mikel*
Cover Design: *Laurie Albrecht*
Typesetting: *Scratchgravel Publishing Services*
Printing and Binding: *Patterson Printing*

For more information, contact:

BROOKS/COLE•WADSWORTH PUBLISHING COMPANY
511 Forest Lodge Road
Pacific Grove, CA 93950
USA

International Thomson Publishing Europe
Berkshire House 168-173
High Holborn
London WC1V 7AA
England

Thomas Nelson Australia
102 Dodds Street
South Melbourne, 3205
Victoria, Australia

Nelson Canada
1120 Birchmount Road
Scarborough, Ontario
Canada M1K 5G4

International Thomson Editores
Seneca 53
Col. Polanco
115060 México, D. F., México

International Thomson Publishing GmbH
Königswinterer Strasse 418
53227 Bonn
Germany

International Thomson Publishing Asia
60 Albert Street
#15-01 Albert Complex
Singapore 189969

International Thomson Publishing Japan
Hirakawacho Kyowa Building, 3F
2-2-1 Hirakawacho
Chiyoda-ku, Tokyo 102
Japan

Printed in the United States of America
10 9 8 7 6 5 4 3 2 1

ISBN 0-534-35557-9

This is dedicated to our families:
Matt, Alec, and Jacob Leibsohn
Mary Anne and Adam Haney

CONTENTS

PART 3

Exercises 51

PREFACE

This project began because we, as counselor educators, wanted a very basic, uncomplicated, and nonthreatening primer for teaching beginning students in our counselor education program. We wanted a text that explained counseling responses in simplified, consistent language. We also wanted a text that emphasized intentionality and focus. Because our students do a great deal of videotaping of their counseling sessions, we wanted a beginning text to have a strong video component and exercises to encourage student interaction. We also felt that this would be useful to other human service and health care programs. It was our intent for the text to stand alone, yet we know the simplicity of this text may warrant the use of other counseling texts, especially theory texts.

We started writing and piloting some ideas in our own beginning counseling skills courses. Feedback from students and teaching assistants refined our ideas. We settled on a model that has 15 counseling responses, three counseling intents, and five areas of focus. We divided the responses into five descriptive categories and came up with a system to help student identify the responses, intents, and focuses.

To create a visual learning tool, we then produced our own video, a large part of which accompanies this worktext in the videocassette and on the CD-ROM. The sessions were unscripted and unrehearsed, though they have been edited for clarity. They were taped in a university-based counselor education program. Current students in a graduate counseling program volunteered to be clients; the young man in sessions 3 and 4 was also a volunteer. We selected the counselors from graduates of this program. In most situations, the counselors and clients did not know each other and had not met as client and counselor prior to taping. We wanted interactions that would encourage discussion about different response options that the counselor could have used, rather than perfect or ideal counseling sessions that could be intimidating to the student. We then developed exercises to be used with the videocassette and, subsequently, the CD-ROM.

Using the videocassette and the exercises, we found that students were able to identify the responses that they were using, their intents, and the focus of each response. We also found that students could decide what type of response was possible, choose an intent and focus, and create an appropriate response. Our enthusiasm about how our students were learning counseling responses led to our wanting to share this with a larger audience.

CD-ROM technology fit perfectly with our belief that this model should be both visual and interactive. Therefore, we produced a CD-ROM. The CD-ROM was designed so that students receive feedback to their input. In promoting the CD-ROM, we are using technology to move the helping professions toward innovative learning systems. It has been quite a challenge to develop this CD-ROM so that it teaches counseling responses in a way that is both basic and effective. The field tests of the CD-ROM have convinced us that it is a valuable learning component.

It is our belief that by knowing what it is like to make a counseling response, and having some understanding of being focused and intentional, students can better incorporate the intricacies of specific techniques and interventions of defined theories relative to different professions. The process of learning counseling responses starts with the basic tools of the profession; just as pencil and pen are tools for the artist, the counselor's tools are *basic counseling responses.* As the student becomes familiar with the basic tools of the art, and learns various ways of using the tools, the student can apply these basics to a structured, scientific system. Thus, intentionality and focus ensure that the counselor is not responding randomly, but rather with a "helping strategy" that can be incorporated into a counseling system.

We struggled with naming the responses, intents, and focuses. We wanted to keep the names simple, have the labels represent the content, and have a common language. We also agree with Kottler and Brown (1996) that "regardless of their work setting, theoretical orientation, training program and client population, counselors all use the same intervention skills" (p. 43). In the end, we chose words that are generic, consistent, and descriptive; we also believe that the 15 basic counseling responses are inclusive of the "intervention skills" that most counselors might use.

The underlying premises of this entire project are:

1. Students learn differently and therefore need choices in how they learn.
2. Teachers teach differently and need a variety of teaching modalities that can be used with flexibility.
3. Modern video and CD-ROM technology can be valuable learning and teaching tools and should be available to the teacher and the student.

With these premises in mind, the worktext, videocassette, and CD-ROM are presented as a package to allow instructors and students different ways and combinations to access, and interact with, the information. The necessary information—primarily the descriptions of the responses, intents, and focuses—is in the worktext and therefore important for completing the exercises, whether in the worktext itself or on the CD-ROM. The videocassette may be used in classrooms and other group learning situations where the tape can be played on VCRs. The CD-ROM may be more appropriate to individual learning if CD-ROM accessibility is available. It is anticipated that CD-ROM accessibility will be as common in the near future as VCRs are today. Thus, the student may use the videocassette today and the CD-ROM in the future.

Seven of the 15 exercises in the worktext are designed to be used with the videocassette; each session on the videocassette, with the respective exercises, is on the CD-ROM. Exercises 8–15 are more advanced and have been designed to be done in a classroom or clinical situation. Since each of the seven video exercises incorporates a transcript used on both the video and the CD-ROM, CD-ROM users can follow the transcripts or use them independently for an additional learning option.

To the Student

This worktext takes you through 15 responses, three intents, and five areas of focus, using descriptions and examples. In addition, 15 exercises allow you to practice this model, seven of them with the videocassette and CD-ROM. The videocassette shows seven counseling sessions with a diversity of clients and counselors. The CD-ROM shows the same counseling sessions as the videocassette, with exercises that are similar but specific to CD-ROM technology. By having both the videocassette and the CD-ROM, individual students, small groups, and larger classes can use whichever is appropriate to the learning situation.

Our goal is for you to be able to identify and use counseling responses as the first step in becoming a counselor or a professional in a related field. This process may be awkward at first, as new language, new concepts, and a different way of communicating are learned. We believe that this model helps ease the awkwardness, while at the same time introducing you to what counseling looks, sounds, and feels like. We think that you will become more comfortable as you move through the exercises described in this worktext.

As you proceed through this worktext, you will read, in Part 1, how this model is organized, understand how counseling intents and focuses can be used with counseling responses, and see how this model compares with other models of counseling. In Part 2, you will find an explanation of the 15 counseling responses and how they have been grouped, with several examples of each. Part 3 of the worktext contains seven exercises to be used with the videocassette and includes transcripts of each of the seven sessions that can be used with both the videocassette and the CD-ROM. In the exercises, complete dialogues between client and counselor show the use of counseling responses in unscripted sessions. Each of the dialogues in this worktext is also on the videocassette and the CD-ROM. Together, the worktext, videocassette, and CD-ROM allow you to read about counseling responses; observe how they are used; identify specific responses, intents, and focuses; and practice the responses in the exercises. You can also compare your identifications with suggested identifications. Reflection questions associated with each exercise encourage further understanding.

To the Instructor

The worktext, CD-ROM, and videocassette can precede the use of more advanced texts on counseling theory and process; they can also be used in conjunction with existing texts in a variety of educational and training situations. The worktext, videocassette, and CD-ROM can be used in a variety of ways. The following are suggestions for their use:

1. The worktext includes information necessary for the completion of all exercises and should be read, discussed, and understood prior to starting the exercises. However, students could observe any of the sessions on the videocassette or CD-ROM prior to reading the text to get a sense of what counseling sessions are like. This option may actually enhance their understanding of the information in the worktext. The order of the 15 basic counseling responses in the worktext reflects a suggested teaching order, but is certainly open to variation. The grouping of the counseling responses is also a way of teaching and learning the responses.

2. The videocassette is designed to accompany the exercises in the worktext; the CD-ROM incorporates the exercises and the sessions that are on the videocassette. We recommend considering the following variables when deciding how to use the videocassette and CD-ROM: (a) available technology, (b) the students' comfort level with technology, and (c) the instructional situation. We encourage instructors to try various combinations to determine what works best for both students and instructor. The CD-ROM is designed primarily for individuals; the videocassette can be used by individuals, in small groups, or for demonstration in a classroom.

3. Exercises 1–7 are explained in the worktext, Part 3, and on the CD-ROM. Exercises 8–15 are explained in the worktext only. We recommend that students start with Exercise 1 and work through Exercise 7. The number of exercises completed, the number of identifications in each exercise completed, and the order of the exercises should be based on such variables as the situation, student developmental levels, student progress, and instructor preferences.

4. Exercises 8–15 are offered for advanced student learning. The counseling interactions for these exercises are done by the students in actual or simulated counseling sessions. The exercises allow students to apply the BCR (basic counseling responses) system of identifying response, intent, and focus to new, unique, student-created sessions. If they are done after Exercises 1–7, students can transfer what they have learned in Exercises 1–7 to their own sessions in 8–15. In a classroom or laboratory situation, Exercises 8–15 can also be practiced in triads. In a triad, students rotate the positions of counselor, client, and observer. Observers watch the session, identify and record counseling responses used in the session, and, in a debriefing session, tell the student/counselor what they observed. This process increases the observation and identification skills of the observer, which are directly transferable to the role of counselor, and gives important feedback to the counselor. Although all of the exercises build upon one another, they can be used in a different order, either partially or completely, or in any other way that meets the diverse teaching and learning situations of counselor education. Students can use the Counselor Response Identification Form (CRIF) in Appendix A for identifying the responses, intents, and focuses for Exercises 8–15.

5. Reflection questions at the end of each exercise encourage students to discuss various variables, including ethnicity, gender, age, disability, and nonverbal responses. Instructors may want to add their own reflection questions.

6. The responses, intents, and focuses identified in the text and exercises by the authors are *only* suggestions. Students and instructors may have different interpretations of what the response, intent, or focus may be. We believe that these differences can lead to constructive discussion, including alternative identifications and alternative counselor responses. Throughout this worktext, emphasis is placed on *comparing* rather than *judging*. Students are continually asked to identify responses, intents, and focuses to compare with the suggested identifications, with the understanding that there are no right and wrong identifications. We believe that this helps students understand that counseling is an art, not a science, and that the way a counselor responds to a client depends on many variables and many interpretations.

7. If other models and theories of counseling are used in a course or program, the terminology and concepts of these models and theories can be applied to the counseling sessions in this system. Table 3 in Appendix A compares the BCR (basic counseling responses) terminology to several other models.

Teaching a beginning counseling course involves more than having an appropriate text. It is recommended that this worktext, CD-ROM, and videocassette be used in concert with:

1. Classroom lectures on various aspects of counseling and the counseling profession. The history of counseling, counseling theories, the current practice of counseling, the distinctions between counseling and therapy, and ethics are topics all counseling courses should include.

2. Demonstration of counseling responses. Instructors should show how various responses are used in a counseling session. Students should be encouraged to practice in the classroom for immediate feedback.
3. Discussions of the use of counseling responses with different clients in different settings. Students should know the cultural and situational variables that influence the use of counseling responses. Specific gender and age issues should be noted.
4. Supplemental texts, journal articles, and related readings.

The format of a counseling course could be as follows:

1. Lecture and discussion on a specific counseling topic.
2. Explanation and demonstration of selected counseling responses.
3. Structured practice session in dyads or triads, preferably videotaped.
4. Feedback sessions with observers and instructors.
5. The use of the BCR exercises or another format for review of practice sessions outside the classroom.
6. Periodic self-reflections and evaluations.

Acknowledgments

Without the inspiration and encouragement of the students of the counseling programs at Seattle University, this project would not have been possible. We are grateful to Anna Fern and Ken Ryan for their extraordinary help with this project and to Helen Shaw for her help with the videocassette. Bill Good and Liz McKinney at Good Northwest have been wonderful partners, as has Nancy Cote. Extra thanks to colleagues Britta Bowman and Joe Afanador. Words cannot describe how rewarding our relationship with Lisa Gebo at Brooks/Cole•Wadsworth has been. Finally, we are grateful to the following reviewers for their comments: Lupe Alle-Corliss, California State University—Fullerton; John A. Casey, University of Nevada, Reno; Molly Davis, George Mason University; Carolyn Dillon, Boston University; Darcy Granello, Ohio State University; David Harvey; Patricia L. Kerstner, University of Phoenix; Cheryl Martin, University of Manitoba; Patrick Romine, University of Phoenix; Walter Swett, Quinsigamond Community College; Mary Swigonski, Monmouth University; Michelle Ventour, Marygrove College; Robert J. Wellman, Fitchburg State College; Matthew Westra, Longview Community College; and Jan Wrenn, Andrews University.

Hutch Haney
Jacqueline Leibsohn

PART 1
Overview

This worktext, which accompanies a videocassette and a CD-ROM, leads the student through a process of learning a new model of counseling that includes 15 counseling *responses*. Associated with each response are three therapeutic *intents* and five *focuses*. The videocassette and CD-ROM exercises help students identify the counseling responses, the intents, the focuses, and their use.

Language

Many authors and practitioners have used the term *counseling skill* to describe what the counselor says to a client. This model uses the term *basic counseling response* to denote each of the 15 counseling responses, for it more accurately describes the process of the counselor's "responding" to the client. The use of the words *counseling* and *counselor* are inclusive of professions where human caregiving is involved; these include, but are not limited to, counseling, social work, pastoral care, nursing, and other health care professions. The counseling responses, intents, and focuses have been named to be as inclusive as possible of other counseling models and generic counseling terminology.

Counseling Response

This model defines 15 basic counseling responses (see Figure 1). Part 2 describes the counseling responses, with several examples of each. Counseling responses are also shown in the videocassette and CD-ROM. The 15 counseling responses are grouped into five categories—essential, passive, active, interpretive, and discretionary—that further define their use. Each counseling response has an associated intent and a focus, described below.

1

FIGURE 1   RESPONSES

OPENING OR CLOSING	ATTENDING	EMPATHIZING
PARAPHRASING	GIVING FEEDBACK	QUESTIONING
CLARIFYING	DIRECTING	PLAYING A HUNCH
NOTING A THEME	NOTING A DISCREPANCY	NOTING A CONNECTION
REFRAMING	ALLOWING	SELF-DISCLOSING

● Intent

This model names three intents (see Figure 2). An intent is the rationale the counselor uses for choosing a given response. Counselors use the responses with the intention:

1. To *acknowledge* the client, thus showing respect and giving the client information through, for example, the responses of *attending* and *giving feedback.*

FIGURE 2   INTENTS

2. To *explore,* thus helping the client gain new information or insight through such responses as *questioning* and *clarifying.*

3. To *challenge* the client to view his or her situation differently or to take alternative action through responses such as *reframing* and *noting a connection.*

Ivey (1994) defines intentionality as

acting with a sense of capability and deciding from among a range of alternative actions. The intentional individual has more than one action, thought, or behavior to choose from in responding to changing life situations. The intentional individual can generate alternatives in a given situation and approach a problem from different vantage points, using a variety of skills and personal qualities, *adapting styles to suit different individuals and cultures.* (p. 11)

By making counseling responses that are designed to *acknowledge,* to *explore,* or to *challenge,* the counselor increases the likelihood that the client will respond in a way that conveys more self-awareness and clarity. Self-awareness and clarity will increase the client's ability to make more informed decisions that, hopefully, will lead to a more fulfilling life.

The counselor's intent may not match the client's experience of the response; the client may hear it differently than the counselor intended. For example, the intent of the counselor may be to *explore:* "Tell me more about that. . . ." However, the client may feel that this response is intended to *challenge.* The counselor needs to be sensitive to how the client perceives the intent of the response.

▼ Focus

Five focuses have been named (see Figure 3). The focus is where the counselor places the emphasis of the counseling response. Counselors do not always focus exclusively on the client; counselors may need information or may need to respond to other people or situations. However, because this model deals with the most basic counseling responses, all 15 responses focus on the client's experience, feelings, thoughts, or behaviors. Immediacy is a focus that can be added to any of the other focuses. It is not a stand-alone focus.

Ivey (1994) describes focusing:

> In your first attempts at practicing interviewing skills, aim to focus your conversation on the client before you, but as you develop increased understanding and skill in the interview, you will want to add broader environmental dimensions to your consideration and planning as well. (p. 15)

The five areas of focus used in this model are:

1. Client experience
2. Client feeling
3. Client thought
4. Client behavior
5. Immediacy

The focus on *client experience* is the broadest response. The counselor keeps his/her response general, allowing the client to choose a more specific area of focus such as a *feeling, thought,* or *behavior.* When the counselor chooses feelings, thoughts, or behaviors, the focus is narrowed. The narrowest focus is *immediacy.* The inverted triangle in Figure 3 shows the narrowing of focus areas.

The additional focus called *immediacy* occurs when the counselor, responding to client experience, client feeling, client thought, or client behavior, encourages the client to focus on the immediate moment. This often means adding "right now" to the counseling response. Immediacy can also be the focus when the counselor focuses on what is currently happening in the client/counselor relationship. To be immediacy-focused means exploring what is happening between the client and the counselor in the *present relationship* or what is being experienced in the *present situation.* The relationship between client and counselor may mirror other relationships or situations, thus giving an immediate picture of how the client interacts with others. To be immediacy-focused can feel challenging to the client. Counselors must be sensitive to clients' reactions to focusing on their present experience and/or the present relationship. Immediacy is concerned with the "here and now aspect of counseling

FIGURE 3   FOCUSES

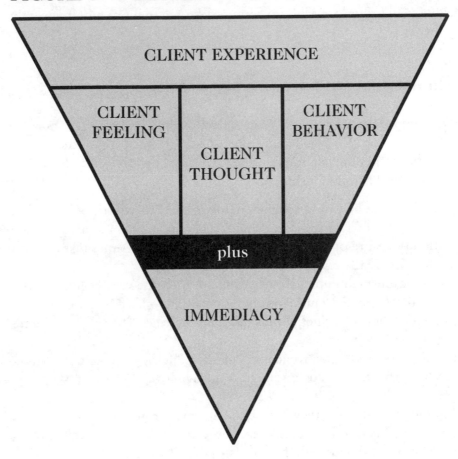

including the therapeutic relationship" (Kottler & Brown, 1996, p. 43). Kleinke (1994) calls this type of response "verbal immediacy":

> When being immediate, the therapist attempts to focus on the therapeutic relationship in the present. There is a sense of directness, intimacy, and willingness to experience with the client what is happening in the moment. (p. 58)

Counseling Defined

Combining the components of this model, counseling can be defined as *an interaction in which the counselor focuses on client experience, client feeling, client thought, and client behavior with intentional responses to acknowledge, to explore, or to challenge.*

Counseling has specific goals, the *first* of which is to facilitate awareness. This is achieved by keeping the focus on the client, acknowledging feelings, experience, and behavior. By exploring feelings and behavior and future options, the *second* counseling goal, healthy decision making, can be maximized. Further exploration and challenging can lead to the *third* goal of counseling, appropriate action, resulting in more fulfilling personal and social functioning.

The Counselor

Most practicing counselors agree that the counseling relationship is critical to client growth. The "personality, values and demeanor" (Okun, 1997, p. 12) of the counselor dictate the forming of a therapeutic relationship. Belkin (1984, pp. 103–104) lists five guidelines necessary for a counseling relationship:

1. The counselor must be willing to listen to *anything* and *everything* the client has to say. The beginning of a constructive counseling relationship requires the counselor to listen without censure or perceptual defense. Clients sometimes test out how carefully or nonjudgmentally the counselor has been listening.
2. The counselor must communicate to the client, from the very beginning, the message, "I am here to *help* you." Counselors sometimes try too hard to communicate, "I want you to like me," but this is not always the right message. The theme of being helpful is more appropriate.
3. Although expressions of positive feelings are helpful, they should be restrained, especially in the early phases of counseling. Avoid giving *any* judgments—even positive ones.
4. Clients progress best when they have to bear some (or most) of the responsibility for the treatment. This attitude is weakened if the counselor takes the role of trying to always reassure the client. It then appears to the client that the burden of successful treatment is on the counselor's shoulders.
5. The counselor should freely and unceremoniously express those feelings and ideas that can help the client grow. When the client sees the counselor talking openly, this communicates the message that the counselor is really interested in him or her as a person.

Concreteness, genuineness, and *respect* are counselor characteristics or attitudes often deemed necessary to fulfill Belkin's guidelines. Concreteness means that the counselor's communication with the client is very clear. This can be accomplished by keeping responses brief and to the point. The "genuine" counselor is true to his/her own beliefs and responds from an understood set of values. To be genuine also means to be self-aware. Above all, the counselor has respect for the client as a person and expresses understanding or the will to understand what the client is experiencing. Egan (1986) describes the "ideal helper" in the following terms:

> They [good helpers] respect their clients and express that *respect* by being available to them, working with them, not judging them, trusting the constructive forces found in them, and ultimately by placing the expectation on them to do whatever is necessary to handle their problems in living more effectively. They *genuinely* care for those who have come for help. They are nondefensive, spontaneous, and always willing to say what they think and feel,

provided it is in the best interest of their clients. Good helpers are *concrete* in their expressions, dealing with actual feelings and actual behavior rather than vague formulations, obscure psychodynamics, or generalities. (p. 29)

A counselor must also be *reflective.* Counselors must "look back" on how they have been with the client; what responses, strategies, and interventions seemed appropriate and useful; and what ethical issues need discernment. The counselor must always ask, "How do I behave as a professional in a helping relationship?" Counselors must also reflect on the counseling intent of their responses. In using this worktext, CD-ROM, and videocassette, counselors are continually asked to reflect upon (1) whether their responses are counseling responses and (2) their relationship with the client within the counseling context. Okun (1997) incorporates the characteristics of the counselor in her definition of counseling:

It is an art in the sense that the personality, values, and demeanor (along with the skills and knowledge) of the counselor are subjective variables in the counseling process that are difficult to define or measure. It is a science in that much of what we know about human behavior and some of the helping strategies has been synthesized into structured, measurable, objective counseling systems. (p. 12)

Counseling, then, depends not just on what the counselor knows or what the counselor says and does, but who the counselor *is.* The exercises in Part 3 encourage students to be knowledgeable about counseling responses *and* to reflect on who they are as reflective, concrete, genuine, and respectful individuals.

Differentiating Response, Intent, and Focus

Throughout the worktext, videocassette, and CD-ROM, and especially in the exercises, students are expected to differentiate the 15 counseling responses, three intents, and five focuses. It is expected that different identifications will be made other than the ones offered as suggestions; this may create ambiguity. As Okun (1997) has noted, counseling is an art, and an art is characteristically ambiguous.

Kottler and Brown (1996) place this issue of ambiguity in the context of the counseling profession itself:

Counseling is indeed an ambiguous enterprise. It is done by persons who can't agree on what to call themselves, what credentials are necessary to practice, or even what is the best way to practice—whether to deal with feelings, thoughts, or behaviors; whether to be primarily supportive or confrontational; whether to focus on the past or the present. (p. 13)

Discussion and debate are encouraged when using this worktext, videocassette, and CD-ROM. Because the counseling relationship is an interpersonal one, personality and culture are significant variables that influence both language and nonverbal communication. Voice inflection, nonverbal behavior, the history of the relationship, and the larger context of the interaction are other variables affecting human interactions. Thus, the suggested responses are just that: *suggested.* They are based on the descriptions in Part 2. While viewing, the student may have a different interpretation. Discussion with others may bring out further interpretations. The importance of possible discrepancies in identifications is that students, their peers, and supervisors are involved in a process of evaluating what the counselor *may* be saying and the *possible* reasons for saying it. Through this process, students can become more focused and intentional as their training continues.

Limitations

This worktext does not include the many issues and concepts related to being a professional counselor. Its purpose is limited to presenting counseling responses in a simplified training format for new counseling students. The responses in this text, CD-ROM, and videocassette are basic to any counseling interaction, at any stage of the counseling process, and are expected to be supplemented in counselor training programs with specific theoretical strategies and interventions. This worktext does not attempt to address the ethical, multicultural, and specific population issues relevant to every counseling situation. It is expected that counselor trainers make every effort to sensitize counselors in training to the ethical, legal, personal and cultural variables affecting the counseling relationship. Two resources that address ethical and multicultural issues, respectively, are *Issues and Ethics in the Helping Professions,* fifth edition, by Gerald Corey, Marianne Schneider Corey, and Patrick Callahan, and *A Theory of Multicultural Counseling and Therapy* by Derald Wing Sue, Allen E. Ivey, and Paul B. Pedersen.

PART 2
Descriptions and Examples

In this section, the 15 basic counseling responses are described and exemplified in the order shown below. In Appendix A, two tables highlight the responses, intents, and focuses. Table 1, Responses and Associated Intents and Focuses, lists the counseling responses and their relationship to the intents and focuses described in Part 1. Table 2, Quick Reference: Responses, Intents, Focuses, gives a short definition and example for each response, intent, and focus.

Types of Responses

The 15 counseling responses are divided into five descriptive groups:

Essential responses
1. Opening or closing
2. Attending

These responses are necessary to all client/counselor interactions.

Passive responses
3. Empathizing
4. Paraphrasing
5. Giving feedback

The counselor gives these responses without expectation of a client response. They show that the counselor is aware of what the client is saying, doing, and feeling.

Active responses
6. Clarifying
7. Directing
8. Questioning

The counselor gives these responses with the expectation that the client will respond with (a) more concrete information or examples, (b) specific requests of the counselor; or (c) answers to the counselor's questions.

Interpretive responses
9. Playing a hunch
10. Noting a theme
11. Noting a discrepancy
12. Noting a connection
13. Reframing

A counselor needs to be familiar with the client's worldview and internal processes in order to offer interpretations. It may take several sessions before the counselor is able to (a) suggest different possibilities, (b) give the counselor's view of the relationships between thoughts, behaviors, and feelings, or (c) offer other interpretive responses.

Discretionary responses
14. Allowing silence
15. Self-disclosing

As a counseling response, self-disclosing should be used with caution because it can risk taking the focus off the client. Allowing silence requires that the counselor be aware of how and when silence can best be used for the client's benefit.

Examples Format

All examples, examples of multiple responses and the extended dialogue in Part 2, as well as the videocassette exercises 1–7 in Part 3, will use the following format:

#	SPEAKER	VERBATIM RESPONSE	IDENTIFICATION
1	COUNSELOR: or CLIENT:	"....dialogue..."	■ RESPONSE ● INTENT ▼ FOCUS

The first column denotes the number of each counselor and client response; multiple counselor responses will have sequential numbers. The second column denotes the speaker, either client or counselor. The third column is the actual dialogue. Counselor and client verbatim responses are in quotes; other information is not. Nonverbal information is in parentheses. The fourth column identifies the basic counseling response, intent, and focus, in that order, with distinctive bullets preceding each (■ for response, ● for intent, and ▼ for focus). Examples will include all counseling responses, intents, and focuses, but some videocassette exercises will not, depending on what is required in the specific exercise. The CD-ROM has its own format for the exercises.

OPENING OR CLOSING

Opening or closing a counseling session is not necessarily considered therapeutic per se, but both may be very important to the entire process and relationship. Openings set the tone and momentum; closings provide closure. Different situations require that different information be given to clients in the first sessions. Generally, clients need to know the qualifications of the counselor, times, dates, and costs, as well as confidentiality parameters. Clients may need an explanation about the counseling process. Meier and Davis (1997) note:

> Clients frequently approach counseling with misconceptions about the process. For example, they may expect counseling to resemble a visit to a medical doctor: diagnosis, prescription, cure. If mistaken expectations are ignored, clients may drop out or fail to make progress. (p. 3)

The opening of a counseling interview can be awkward for both client and counselor. Clients are understandably cautious about sharing their lives with a new person. Tension and anxiety are a natural response to new situations; thus resistance is very common. Counselors are encouraged to be very patient, especially in the initial interview. Reducing the initial tension may not necessarily be the goal of the counselor. The counselor needs to decide what his/her views are regarding the optimal level of anxiety. It is generally agreed that giving some structure to the initial session helps the client feel safe and promotes trust. Giving clients initial choices can reduce the anxiety: "Where would you like to sit?"

It is generally assumed to be the counselor's responsibility to decide when the session begins (after the client sits down, for example, rather than in the hall walking to the office). A common phrase of a counselor to start a session is "Where would you like to start?" This phrase puts the choice and responsibility on the client.

Counselors can assume the responsibility for closing a session, though this, too, can be given to the client. Some counselors have clocks or hourglasses and let the clients know that it is their responsibility to pace themselves and end the session on time. Ending on time is almost always essential, given time constraints of both counselor and client, and many theorists believe that it is important for clients to learn to work in a specific time frame. A common phrase is "We have five minutes left, how would you like to close?" Opening or closing can be in question or statement form.

The ending of the client/counselor relationship is also important because it may mirror the ending of other relationships. Counselors should allow ample time to process the ending of this relationship and can use questions to *challenge* as closing responses: "How has our time together been for you?" or "How is it to end our relationship?"

Generally, the intent of opening is to *explore* what the client may want to discuss. The intent of closing is generally to *acknowledge* the end of a session. Opening or closing responses may focus on client experience, client feeling, client thought, and/or client behavior.

11

Since most responses of this type are open-ended to allow the client to choose the specific focus, the focus is *primarily* on client experience. Although opening or closing refers to the immediate situation, it does not have an immediacy focus unless the counselor specifically adds it, as in "How is it to end at this moment?"

Examples of Opening or Closing

EXAMPLE 1 (OPENING)

#	SPEAKER	VERBATIM RESPONSE	IDENTIFICATION
1.1	COUNSELOR:	"Where would you like to begin today?"	■ OPENING OR CLOSING ● TO EXPLORE ▼ CLIENT EXPERIENCE

EXAMPLE 2 (OPENING)

#	SPEAKER	VERBATIM RESPONSE	IDENTIFICATION
2.1	COUNSELOR:	"What would you like to talk about today?"	■ OPENING OR CLOSING ● TO EXPLORE ▼ CLIENT EXPERIENCE

EXAMPLE 3 (CLOSING)

#	SPEAKER	VERBATIM RESPONSE	IDENTIFICATION
3.1	COUNSELOR:	"We have five minutes left."	■ OPENING OR CLOSING ● TO ACKNOWLEDGE ▼ CLIENT EXPERIENCE

EXAMPLE 4 (CLOSING)

#	SPEAKER	VERBATIM RESPONSE	IDENTIFICATION
4.1	COUNSELOR:	"This seems like a good place to stop for today."	■ OPENING OR CLOSING ● TO ACKNOWLEDGE ▼ CLIENT EXPERIENCE
4.2	CLIENT:	"Um . . . I'm so tired . . . it actually feels good to have just gotten all that said and out in the open, and it feels now like sort of a relief. I just want to go home and go to bed."	

#	SPEAKER	VERBATIM RESPONSE	IDENTIFICATION
4.3	COUNSELOR:	"I'll see you next week."	

Other counseling responses can be used to start or to end a session: simple greetings, directing ("Let's start where we left off last week"; "Let's stop here"), gestures, paraphrasing ("Well, you called and made an appointment and said you wanted to discuss something with me"), and allowing silence are often used, especially in a relationship in which both counselor and client are familiar with the process.

2 ATTENDING

*A*ttending means giving undivided attention to the client. It is the art of being with the client. It is also the art of paying attention to what you see and hear rather than what you know. Being attended to—being heard—helps the client and encourages self-reflection.

It is important to give the client plenty of time and space. Thus, part of attending is to slow the pace, resisting the temptation to talk or to keep the conversation moving. It is also important to allow for silences, again resisting the temptation to fill the voids of a conversation.

Attending, like many things in counseling, is different from conversation in social or work situations. Counselors must refrain from learned behaviors such as talking about oneself, asking a lot of questions, and avoiding lulls and silences. Thus, while attending may seem simple, it actually can be difficult, for it requires that the counselor truly pay attention to what the client is saying and doing, rather than what the counselor is thinking. Attending is something that counselors do all the time with all clients and thus is an integral part of every counseling response. Attending is mostly nonverbal (such as maintaining appropriate eye contact and an open posture), though the counselor may utter an occasional "uh-huh" or "mm." Being attentive also shows respect and caring.

Attending also means observing. Counselors must observe in their clients both verbal and nonverbal behavior. Ivey (1994) says,

> Client observation skills enable you to note and understand clients' behavior in the interview and their patterns of discussing key situations. This understanding will help you choose useful interviewing skills and counseling interventions to facilitate client growth and development. (p. 69)

Attending is usually intended to *acknowledge* the client. The counselor may focus on feelings, thoughts, or behaviors, but since this is a nonverbal response, it is usually focused on the experience of being with the client in the situation.

Examples of Attending

EXAMPLE 1

#	SPEAKER	VERBATIM RESPONSE	IDENTIFICATION
1.1	CLIENT:	"I've been kind of testing the waters to see what they would do in my situation."	
1.2	COUNSELOR:	"Uh-hum."	■ ATTENDING ● TO ACKNOWLEDGE ▼ CLIENT EXPERIENCE

#	SPEAKER	VERBATIM RESPONSE	IDENTIFICATION
1.3	CLIENT:	"But it is really my decision to make."	

EXAMPLE 2

#	SPEAKER	VERBATIM RESPONSE	IDENTIFICATION
2.1	COUNSELOR:	When the client made some more serious remarks about recent feelings of self-doubt, the counselor's response was to lean forward.	■ ATTENDING ● TO ACKNOWLEDGE ▼ CLIENT EXPERIENCE

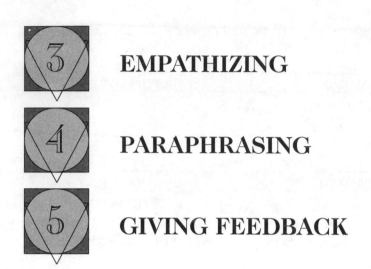

3 EMPATHIZING

4 PARAPHRASING

5 GIVING FEEDBACK

Paraphrasing, summarizing, reflecting, reflection of feeling, reflection of content, mirroring, parroting, and *empathizing* are terms used by various counselor educators to denote counseling responses that (1) let the client know the counselor is listening and (2) reflect what the counselor has seen or heard. Okun (1997) defines reflecting as

> communicating to the helpee our understanding of his or her concerns and perspectives. We can reflect stated or implied feelings, what we have observed nonverbally, what we feel has been omitted or emphasized, and specific content. (p. 75)

Generally, paraphrasing and summarizing are ways of telling clients what the counselor heard them say, in the counselor's words. Summarizing is the same as paraphrasing, but generally covers more information, such as the complete session, rather than one or two client responses. Empathizing, or reflection of feelings, adds the counselor's sense of what the client is feeling. Giving feedback is stating to the client what the counselor observes. These responses each have a respective focus:

* *Empathizing* is a response to *client feeling.*
* *Paraphrasing* is a response to *client experience, client thought,* and/or *client behavior.*
* *Giving feedback* is a response to observed *client behavior.*

An example of paraphrasing is "You are saying . . ." or "What I hear you saying is . . ." An example of empathizing is "You feel . . ." A counselor giving feedback could say, "I notice tears in your eyes as you are talking" or "You have used the word 'control' several times."

Generally, the intent of all three responses is to acknowledge, though naming the intent or the response can be ambiguous. For example, the counselor says, "I notice that you are smiling while you are talking about feeling sad." Although this sounds like giving feedback to acknowledge client behavior and empathizing to acknowledge feelings, the intent is most likely to challenge the discrepancy between the feelings and the observed behavior. Therefore, this response is actually noting a discrepancy to challenge client feeling and client behavior.

The three sections that follow give explanations and examples of each of the three passive responses: empathizing, paraphrasing, and giving feedback.

Empathizing

Empathizing requires that the counselor be able to join with the client and try to understand how it feels to be that individual, with all the client's unique qualities and perspectives. At the same time, it is important that the counselor remain separate from the client's experience. If this is done successfully, the client will feel understood at a core level. This is a very different experience from what the client might get from a friend. Usually a friend will say, "I know exactly how you feel," whereas a counselor responds, "You're feeling sad."

Empathizing about client feelings requires that the counselor have some understanding of the client's feelings even though the counselor may not have actually had the same feeling. The counselor may, in fact, *not* understand the client's feelings or experience or behavior. This is okay! The important aspect of being empathetic is the *desire* to understand and the ability to communicate that desire. The counselor can always ask, "Am I understanding you correctly?" The counselor can check with the client whether the counselor is understanding him/her; if not, then the client can clarify his/her own understanding (one of the goals of counseling) and at the same time know that the counselor cares enough to try to understand.

Egan (1994) defines empathy in this way:

> Empathy as a form of human communication involves listening to clients, understanding them and their concerns to the degree that this is possible, and communicating this understanding to them so that they might understand themselves more fully and act on their understanding. (p. 106)

Egan (1994) distinguishes between empathy and "advanced empathy . . . where the counselor goes beyond the expressed, the partially expressed and the implied" (p. 212). In the BCR model, Egan's concept of advanced empathy is broken down into several responses: noting a connection, noting a theme, and playing a hunch (see descriptions and examples of these responses later in the text).

Reflection of feelings is a term that has been used for the expression of empathy and is another way of showing that the counselor is aware of the client's feelings: "You feel sad."

Empathizing with client feelings is also expressed nonverbally. A client may be talking about a painful experience while clutching his/her throat; the counselor, by imitating the gesture, shows that the counselor understands the pain.

Examples of Empathizing

EXAMPLE 1

#	SPEAKER	VERBATIM RESPONSE	IDENTIFICATION
1.1	CLIENT:	"You know, I haven't heard from any of them, and if they are not too busy, then they could at least call me."	
1.2	COUNSELOR:	"You feel forgotten, left out."	■ EMPATHIZING ● TO ACKNOWLEDGE ▼ CLIENT FEELING

EXAMPLE 2

#	SPEAKER	VERBATIM RESPONSE	IDENTIFICATION
2.1	CLIENT:	"Now I feel like I'm getting a cold, and I'm thinking, oh no, who needs this now . . . (short pause) . . . and who will take care of me . . . (short pause) . . . no one will (pause) . . . so I guess I'm feeling sorry for myself."	
2.2	COUNSELOR:	"You feel alone; there is no one there to take care of you when you need it."	■ EMPATHIZING ● TO ACKNOWLEDGE ▼ CLIENT FEELING

Paraphrasing

Paraphrasing what the client is telling the counselor is usually a sentence or two used throughout the session: "This is what I heard you saying . . ." or "You *are* telling me that . . ." The essential feature is to let the client hear what the essence of his/her statement is. It is important to restate some of the client's own words, but with additional words of the counselor to help let the client know that the counselor truly hears what the client is saying. Kleinke (1994) describes paraphrasing as follows:

> A paraphrase is a rephrasing of the client's statement in a way that communicates to the client the therapist's understanding of what the client has said. The paraphrase is used to focus the communication on issues that appear to be most relevant and appropriate. When paraphrasing, therapists don't simply parrot or repeat the client's exact words. By making an active attempt to rephrase the client's statement in their own words, therapists are able to maintain the flow and focus of the conversation. (p. 61)

A longer paraphrase, or summary, can also be given at the end of a session or to transition to a new topic—for example, "You *have said* that . . ." to transition to a new topic or to end a session. Paraphrasing differs from giving feedback in that giving feedback generally notes specific words or phrases that the client has used that the counselor wants to highlight.

Examples of Paraphrasing

EXAMPLE 1

#	SPEAKER	VERBATIM RESPONSE	IDENTIFICATION
1.1	CLIENT:	"Ya know, my father isn't such a bad guy. He tries hard, but his life is tough. Sometimes when he comes home from work he's drunk. Then no one knows what to do. Should we be quiet? Should we be happy and greet him? We never know what to do."	

#	SPEAKER	VERBATIM RESPONSE	IDENTIFICATION
1.2	COUNSELOR:	"When your father comes home drunk, you don't know what he'll be like, so you don't know how to act."	■ PARAPHRASING ● TO ACKNOWLEDGE ▼ CLIENT BEHAVIOR
1.3	CLIENT:	"Yes, that's it. It's so hard. I never know what to do, and it's scary."	

EXAMPLE 2

#	SPEAKER	VERBATIM RESPONSE	IDENTIFICATION
2.1	CLIENT:	"When I'm angry with my friend, I just change the subject or walk away."	
2.2	COUNSELOR:	"You don't tell your friend when you are mad at her."	■ PARAPHRASING ● TO ACKNOWLEDGE ▼ CLIENT BEHAVIOR
2.3	CLIENT:	"Right. I don't want her to know."	

Giving Feedback

Giving feedback regarding the client's verbal or nonverbal behavior is simply telling the client what you see and hear while you are together: "I see that you are smiling"; "I heard your voice crack when you said 'daughter' "; "I notice that your arms have been crossed most of the session."

In some contexts, outside of the counseling relationship, giving feedback is seen as person A telling person B what A thinks or feels about B, whether in terms of personality characteristics, job performance, or test results. Guidelines to giving feedback in a counseling relationship include owning the feedback, being positive and specific, noting behavior not personal traits, and not putting the person receiving the feedback on the defensive. In this model, giving feedback is only the act of sharing precisely what the counselor has heard or observed.

Most often, the information given back to the client is not new to the client. Sometimes, because of the focus of attention on the statement or behavior, the information may feel new, thus increasing the client's self-awareness. Receiving feedback may be threatening, or the person may not see the feedback as increasing self-awareness. Therefore, it may be important to follow up with, "How was it for you to get this feedback?" (questioning to challenge with the focus on the client experience plus immediacy) .

Giving feedback about specific, observed behavior is different from paraphrasing about the client's feelings or experiences. The counselor is reiterating a specific observation, rather than encapsulating, using the counselor's wording, what has been said by the client.

Examples of Giving Feedback

EXAMPLE 1

#	SPEAKER	VERBATIM RESPONSE	IDENTIFICATION
1.1	CLIENT:	"My life is real full. Full with my wife and children, work, home, activities, (pause) then my dad. . . . He's getting older, and I don't see him as much as before."	
1.2	COUNSELOR:	"Your voice got quiet when you said 'older.'"	■ GIVING FEEDBACK ● TO ACKNOWLEDGE ▼ CLIENT BEHAVIOR
1.3	CLIENT:	"Ya, he's looking real old. I don't know . . ."	

EXAMPLE 2

#	SPEAKER	VERBATIM RESPONSE	IDENTIFICATION
2.1	CLIENT:	"I feel isolated, like I'm an island. There are no other people on this island. No one will ever find this island."	
2.2	COUNSELOR:	"I heard you say 'I'm an island.'"	■ GIVING FEEDBACK ● TO ACKNOWLEDGE ▼ CLIENT BEHAVIOR

6 CLARIFYING

Clarifying is a response from the counselor to encourage clients to be clear about what they are truly feeling and experiencing. As a result, clients become more aware, and less vague. Many clients will use generalizations and abstract notions to keep the focus off themselves and defend against anxiety. As the counselor asks the client to clarify and be more concrete, these defenses are confronted. The counselor asks the client to clarify; it is *not* the counselor's job to do the clarifying for the client. According to Egan (1986), "problem situations are clarified if they are spelled out in terms of specific and relevant experiences, behaviors, and feelings" (pp. 169–170).

If the counselor is unclear about what the client is saying, the client may also be unclear. The counselor should not make any assumptions. Therefore, asking for clarification can be for both the client and the counselor. A client may say, "I'm depressed." The counselor should not assume that either the client or the counselor understands what this means and should ask for clarification—for example, "What do you mean by depressed?"

Initially, clarifying should be used with caution to avoid interrupting and distracting. Later, especially in the planning and action phases of counseling, it may be necessary to clarify often and to encourage exactness.

Though it may be a challenge for clients to clarify their responses, the intent of the counselor is almost always to *explore* a vague or incomplete statement by the client. The focus of clarifying is on client experience, client feeling, client thought, or client behavior. However, in clarifying responses, the words of the counselor may not indicate focus, because they often refer only to what the client is saying. Often the client is talking about an experience, and to encourage clarification of the broader experience, the counselor will respond with a narrower focus on feelings, thoughts, or behaviors.

Asking the client to clarify can also be done by requesting that the client tell you *more* about what he/she is talking about. It is not asking specifically for more concrete or specific information. Such clarifying responses may be in the form of a question, "Will you tell me *more* about that?" or a statement—short words such as "uh-huh," nods of the head, or short sentences or phrases such as "Tell me more about that" (note that this may sound like directing, or telling the client what to do, but it does not ask for a change of direction or for something new), or words that trail such as "and . . ." or "and then . . ." This type of clarifying response encourages clients to disclose information about themselves and indicates a willingness on the part of the counselor to listen. The intent of this type of clarifying is to encourage clients to tell *more*—that is, to expand on what they are saying. Egan (1994) uses the terms *probe* and *prompt* for eliciting information and encouraging the client to discuss an issue more fully.

> Prompts and probes are verbal tactics for helping clients talk about themselves and define their concerns more concretely in terms of specific experiences, behaviors, and feelings and the themes that emerge from an exploration of these. (p. 122)

Following are examples of clarifying responses that encourage the client to expand and those that encourage the client to be more specific.

Examples of Clarifying That Encourage Expansion

EXAMPLE 1

#	SPEAKER	VERBATIM RESPONSE	IDENTIFICATION
1.1	CLIENT:	"I'm so concerned about my son. I try to help, so I call him a lot and try to be there. . . ."	
1.2	COUNSELOR:	"And . . ."	■ CLARIFYING ● TO EXPLORE ▼ CLIENT FEELING
1.3	CLIENT:	"I'm afraid I'll drive him away."	

EXAMPLE 2

#	SPEAKER	VERBATIM RESPONSE	IDENTIFICATION
2.1	CLIENT:	"As I started to put it into context, it feels less heavy. It still feels challenging and somewhat intimidating. . . . It doesn't feel quite as heavy (silence for approximately 20 seconds). The whole matter of childhood tapes . . ."	
2.2	COUNSELOR:	"Tell me more. . . ."	■ CLARIFYING ● TO EXPLORE ▼ CLIENT FEELING
2.3	CLIENT:	"Suddenly one starts hearing voices from those old tapes and there is something around the issue of perfectionism. . . . I've been trying to get a better sense of where that stuff comes from."	

Examples of Clarifying
That Encourage More Specificity

EXAMPLE 3

#	SPEAKER	VERBATIM RESPONSE	IDENTIFICATION
3.1	CLIENT:	"But it's quite a responsibility being a parent. You look back at all the mistakes. . . . I feel good about the communication between me and my kids."	
3.2	COUNSELOR:	"Can you tell me more about the 'responsibility'?"	■ CLARIFYING ● TO EXPLORE ▼ CLIENT THOUGHT
3.3	CLIENT:	"Yeah, the responsibility is overwhelming at times. When you look at how each kid is different, and how you want each kid to be . . . healthy, getting a good education, choosing good friends."	

EXAMPLE 4

#	SPEAKER	VERBATIM RESPONSE	IDENTIFICATION
4.1	CLIENT:	"I'm feeling real vulnerable today."	
4.2	COUNSELOR:	"When you say you're feeling vulnerable, can you be more specific?"	■ CLARIFYING ● TO EXPLORE ▼ CLIENT FEELING
4.3	CLIENT:	"It's like everyone knows how I feel . . . like I can be hurt easily."	

Note: After a client has been more concrete, as in the previous example, the counselor often has a hunch about the client's feelings and can respond by playing a hunch: "Sounds to me like you might also be mad." This would be done with the intent to challenge client feeling.

DIRECTING

As the counseling relationship becomes more trusting and rapport has been established, it may be appropriate for the counselor to be directive. To be directive is to ask the client to do something new or different or to go in a different direction. The counselor may ask the client to go back to something that was said earlier, or to stop and stay with an emotion. Giving homework is another way of directing. When asking the client to respond to a specific direction, the counselor should be mindful of the client's reaction to the directive. The counselor should be respectful of the client's willingness and readiness to engage in the activity.

To be directive is not to ask for more information, though that may often sound like a directive—for example, "Tell me more" (clarifying). Questioning or clarifying responses with the intent to explore, asked following the carrying out of a directive, can help the client understand and internalize the impact of what was asked. For example, the counselor can say, "How was it for you to do this exercise?" or "Tell me how it is when I ask you to stay with this."

Ivey (1994) notes the simplicity and commonality of directing:

> To give a directive you simply tell the client what to do, what action to take, or what to say or think next. Many of those who take the position that interviewers should not direct their clients fail to address the fact that an interviewer often tells the client to take a test, to free-associate from a dream, to try a new behavior with spouse or colleague, or to engage in some productive homework. (p. 271)

Directing is usually done with the intent to *explore* or to *challenge.* By asking the client to engage in a new activity, the counselor may be intending that the client explore an area of interest or further explore a current situation, behavior, or feeling. The result of the direction can be quite challenging for the client, and that may also be the intent of the counselor's directive. Asking the client to dialogue with an empty chair will most often challenge the client to consider different thoughts, beliefs, feelings, or behaviors.

Specific interventions associated with specific counseling theories are generally used at the direction of the counselor:

1. A more behavioral example of directing is for the counselor to say, "Before you return next week, I want you to make a list of things that make you angry." Thus, the counselor gives the client a specific instruction in the belief that completing the "assignment" will benefit the client.
2. To use the Gestalt technique of the "empty chair," the counselor becomes a "director," instructing the client to play various roles and make certain responses.

Examples of Directing

EXAMPLE 1

#	SPEAKER	VERBATIM RESPONSE	IDENTIFICATION
1.1	CLIENT:	(Speaking about his job) "Why am I doing this to myself? Just for money? I'm prostituting myself. It doesn't make you feel good if you think about it." (The client continues to talk about work issues.)	
1.2	COUNSELOR:	"Let's go back to something you said: 'Why am I doing this to myself?'"	■ DIRECTING ● TO EXPLORE ▼ CLIENT EXPERIENCE
1.3	CLIENT:	"It's a good question. Yeah. Why am I doing this? It's obvious. Benefits and money. The purpose is gone now. I don't need the money anymore. I don't need the benefits. . . . I have some coverage from my partner."	

EXAMPLE 2

#	SPEAKER	VERBATIM RESPONSE	IDENTIFICATION
2.1	COUNSELOR:	"Let's imagine you are talking to your supervisor now. What do you hear yourself saying to her?"	■ DIRECTING ● TO CHALLENGE ▼ CLIENT THOUGHT
2.2	CLIENT:	"I'm going to discuss the parking issue. I'm going to assert myself with my supervisor with fairness around these two parking places. With my supervisor's help, we will decide together how best to approach this woman. I can talk to this woman with my supervisor present, or I can talk to this woman with her supervisor and my supervisor present."	

8 QUESTIONING

Q*uestioning* can challenge clients to evaluate whether behaviors, thoughts, or feelings are effective in getting them what they want—for example, "Is this working for you?" "How" questions often evoke responses in which the client has to reflect upon new or existing information. When a client presents feelings that differ from one week to the next, a counselor could ask, "How is this week different from last week?"

Kleinke (1994) describes four kinds of questions and gives an example of each:

1. Linear questions are necessary for completing a basic assessment of a client's problems.

    "What problems are troubling you?"

2. Exploratory questions that attempt to identify patterns and connections between a client's problems and his or her coping styles, ways of thinking, and interpersonal relationships are called circular questions.

    "What kinds of situations make you particularly anxious?"

3. Strategic questions may successfully challenge clients to change their behaviors or ways of thinking.

    "Why haven't you told your wife how unhappy you are?"

4. Reflective questions enable the client to generate and consider new possibilities.

    "What might be some specific benefits of taking more responsibility for your life?" (pp. 63–64)

Asking questions to get information is a response that most people have mastered. The counselor, however, should have a therapeutic intent: to *acknowledge,* to *explore,* or to *challenge* the client, rather than just to get information. Most questioning as a counseling response is done with the intent to challenge. "How" questions are usually open-ended: "How do you feel about that?" "Why" questions are also open-ended but require a rational explanation and can put clients on the defense. Counselors are encouraged not to ask double questions: "Is it hard for you to both work and study, and how does your family feel about this?" Note that this question is not only double, but the focus is both on the client and on other people; it also asks for a feeling response and for information. Counselors are also encouraged not to ask a question and then give a multiple-choice answer; this inhibits client exploration. For example, "How do you feel about that—sad, confused, angry . . . ?"

Refraining from asking questions is not easy. The counselor needs to know the importance of timing—when to ask a question, and when not to ask a question. Timing is learned by having some understanding of the therapeutic value of the question and the anticipated response from the client.

Clients often do not respond to the counselor's question. The counselor, if he/she wants the client to respond to the question, may need to follow up by repeating the question or giving feedback: "I notice that you did not respond to my question."

Although questioning is named as a distinct basic counseling response, other basic counseling responses can take the form of a question—for example, "How would you like to start the session?" (opening) or "Can you be more specific or give an example?" (clarifying).

Questions can be either open-ended or closed-ended. An open-ended question generally elicits two or three sentences; closed-ended questions can usually be answered with one or two words. As a counseling response, an open-ended question usually evokes more exploration. The focus can be on client feeling, client experience, or client behavior, as well as immediacy.

Examples of Questioning

EXAMPLE 1

#	SPEAKER	VERBATIM RESPONSE	IDENTIFICATION
1.1	CLIENT:	The client had been discussing how she had difficulties controlling her emotional responses earlier in the session and feelings of lack of control. The client later reported that she was "comfortable with it and that it was okay unless it became a problem."	
1.2	COUNSELOR:	"How could it be a problem for you now?"	■ QUESTIONING ● TO CHALLENGE ▼ CLIENT EXPERIENCE
1.3	CLIENT:	"I guess I am okay with it all the time in the ways that I've experienced it in the past, but my concern now is how to still not box myself away from what is a genuine response."	

EXAMPLE 2

#	SPEAKER	VERBATIM RESPONSE	IDENTIFICATION
2.1	CLIENT:	The client tells the counselor that she has dropped two of her classes to spend more time with her kids.	
2.2	COUNSELOR:	"How are you feeling about your decision?"	■ QUESTIONING ● TO CHALLENGE ▼ CLIENT FEELING

Examples of Questioning with an Immediacy Focus

EXAMPLE 3

#	SPEAKER	VERBATIM RESPONSE	IDENTIFICATION
3.1	COUNSELOR:	The counselor has asked the client to summarize the session.	
3.2	CLIENT:	"I don't want to summarize."	
3.3	COUNSELOR:	"Are you annoyed with me right now for asking you to summarize?"	■ QUESTIONING ● TO CHALLENGE ▼ CLIENT FEELING plus IMMEDIACY

EXAMPLE 4

#	SPEAKER	VERBATIM RESPONSE	IDENTIFICATION
4.1	CLIENT:	"It means they went on a lunch break (client giggles), and I'm feeling really vulnerable (pause), so they're not there to build the walls of protection for me."	
4.2	COUNSELOR:	"What does that feel like right now that you have no wall of protection?"	■ QUESTIONING ● TO CHALLENGE ▼ CLIENT FEELING plus IMMEDIACY

PLAYING A HUNCH

To play a hunch requires that a level of trust has been established between the client and the counselor, and that the counselor trusts his/her intuitive sense of what *might* be going on. *Playing a hunch* is used to lead to a deeper understanding of the client's issues, feelings, or situation, and the meaning that the client gives to these. Thus, over a period of time, the counselor forms an interpretation, shares it with the client, encourages the processing of this new information, and, when appropriate, asks the client to reflect on the experience of processing the new information. A hunch does not have to be accurate; a hunch is what the counselor feels, and may not be what the client feels. The importance of a hunch is to give the client an opportunity to react to some new information.

Egan (1985) states,

> Advanced empathy described most simply means sharing hunches about clients and their overt and covert experiences, behaviors, and feelings that you feel will help them see their problems and concerns more clearly and help them move on to developing new scenarios, setting goals, and acting. (p. 79)

The intent is to *challenge* the client. The focus can be on client experience, client feeling, client thought, and/or client behavior, and can have an immediacy focus. Hunches can be "played" with tentativeness because they are interpretations and often confrontational.

Examples of Playing a Hunch

EXAMPLE 1

#	SPEAKER	VERBATIM RESPONSE	IDENTIFICATION
1.1	CLIENT:	"But I do think that, too, that I know that I need someone to lean on, too, and that I need to do these things, too."	
1.2	COUNSELOR:	"So, I sense some resentment because you do get called on by family members. You're the one that people look to lean on, and yet I hear you maybe thinking, "But what about me?""	■ PLAYING A HUNCH ● TO CHALLENGE ▼ CLIENT FEELING

EXAMPLE 2

#	SPEAKER	VERBATIM RESPONSE	IDENTIFICATION
2.1	CLIENT:	The client has been talking about how the corporation once had "things going well for them," "good for them," "the bucks were rolling in," and how negative it is now.	
2.2	COUNSELOR:	"I'm wondering, after hearing you talk about this, whether it's a possibility that you feel very undervalued, that people don't care about you at work—the higher-ups, the corporation does not acknowledge you as a person."	■ PLAYING A HUNCH ● TO CHALLENGE ▼ CLIENT EXPERIENCE and CLIENT FEELING
2.3	CLIENT:	"Oh, I definitely feel that way. I think most of us feel that way, and express it almost daily. But more than that, I understand the rules of the game. . . . It's just at this point, I'm building toward something else. At the same time, I'm beating myself up making a living there. I wish I could just end it and drop the ax on them. They'd just love that."	

Example of Playing a Hunch with an Immediacy Focus

EXAMPLE 3

#	SPEAKER	VERBATIM RESPONSE	IDENTIFICATION
3.1	CLIENT:	The client had been talking about his family and friends who live at a distance. When we got close to talking about how he was feeling, he asked how much time was left. There was a long pause.	
3.2	COUNSELOR	"It seems like you are missing them right now as you sit here with me."	■ PLAYING A HUNCH ● TO CHALLENGE ▼ CLIENT FEELING plus IMMEDIACY

NOTING A THEME

A counselor often looks for themes or patterns that run through the session or a series of sessions: themes of interacting, behaving, thinking, and feeling. For example, the counselor might point out that whenever the client gets into difficult situations he/she tries to escape, run away, or leave the situation. This would be a pattern noticed over a period of time. *Noting a theme* needs to be clearly stated and thus can be confrontational; as with other responses that require that the counselor be more interpretive, tentative language can be used. The intent of noting a theme could be to acknowledge or to explore, but most often it is to *challenge* the client. Counselors may choose to use the word *theme* or *pattern,* rather than just responding to what has been heard, which may be closer to the response of paraphrasing. Noting a theme is not just pointing out a common denominator or a repeated topic, but impressing on the client the significance of the frequent occurrence of a theme that the client may not be aware of. According to Egan (1994), who considers the identifying of themes as part of advanced empathy,

> Helping clients identify and explore themes that emerge in their discussions of problem situations and unused opportunities, especially self-defeating themes, is critical. . . . Once you see a self-defeating theme or pattern emerging from your discussions, your task is to communicate your perception to the client in a way that enables the client to check it out. (pp. 182–183)

Examples of Noting a Theme

EXAMPLE 1

#	SPEAKER	VERBATIM RESPONSE	IDENTIFICATION
1.1	CLIENT:	"This paper has a life of its own. I've created a monster from it. I want it to be perfect, but I can't seem to get it right. I see it as a separate entity that is totally burning me up. I'm creating my own anxiety."	
1.2	COUNSELOR:	"I've heard this theme in previous sessions: You have high expectations of yourself and then you don't expect to meet them."	■ NOTING A THEME ● TO CHALLENGE ▼ CLIENT THOUGHT

31

#	SPEAKER	VERBATIM RESPONSE	IDENTIFICATION
1.3	CLIENT:	"Yeah. This seems to be a major part of my life! It's really annoying and frustrating. I haven't been able to get past it. But it is a pattern."	

EXAMPLE 2

#	SPEAKER	VERBATIM RESPONSE	IDENTIFICATION
2.1	CLIENT:	"There's a friend coming in from California and so I'll probably do something fun and not even remember Father's Day."	
2.2	COUNSELOR:	"I want to note that your relationship with your father is a theme that comes up again and again."	■ NOTING A THEME ● TO CHALLENGE ▼ CLIENT BEHAVIOR
2.3	CLIENT:	"Well, I'm not celebrating Father's Day anyway so it doesn't matter. I'll just not even think about it. I don't want to talk about my father, and I'm tired of always having to deal with how I feel about him."	

NOTING A DISCREPANCY

Discrepancies, or apparent discrepancies, are pointed out by the counselor from what the counselor has observed and surmised. In other words, the counselor goes beyond what the client has recently said and suggests that there may be a discrepancy in what the client is now saying, has said before, or is doing. Ivey (1994) uses the term *confrontation* as the skill the counselor uses to point out discrepancies. Ivey says: "Confrontation may be briefly defined as noting discrepancies in the client and feeding them back via attending skills" (p. 190).

Lauver and Harvey (1997) also use the term *confrontation* in relation to discrepancies: "The counselor-perceived discrepancy in client behavior is a cue for counselor confrontation" (p. 86).

Thus, like other interpretive responses that present new information or known information in a new way, *noting a discrepancy* may be intentionally confrontative on the counselor's part and be perceived as a confrontation on the client's part. Being sensitive to how receptive a client is to a confrontation, the counselor may vary how the response is said. For example, the counselor may say, "I notice that a few minutes ago you said that you wanted to change; now you are saying that you do not want to change." Note that *but* was not used, which makes this confrontation "softer." A "harder" confrontation may be used when a softer confrontation has not been recognized—for example: "You said that you wanted to change, but now you are saying. . . ." Note that *but* was used. In both of these examples, the discrepancy is implied. Although the response may actually sound like giving feedback or paraphrasing, the counselor's intent—that is, to challenge rather than to acknowledge—is what defines the noting-a-discrepancy response. Stronger use of this response may entail actually using the word *discrepancy;* for example, "I see a discrepancy between. . . ." A slightly softer response may use tentativeness: "It seems that there may be a discrepancy between. . . ."

Noting a discrepancy means that the counselor must trust his/her own awareness and the client's ability to process the apparent discrepancy. It is helpful to follow up a discrepancy with an opportunity for the client to discuss the impact of having the discrepancy noted: "How was it to have this pointed out?" (questioning with the intent to challenge).

Discrepancies may include differences between

1. What a client is saying or *not* saying and the counselor's perception of what the client is experiencing.
2. What the client is saying and what the counselor heard the client say at another time.
3. What the client is saying in the session and the client's actions outside the session.
4. What the client is saying that is not congruent with the client's behavior.

Because a discrepancy usually involves two components, counselors often use both hands ("On one hand . . . , on the other . . .") to express these two components. This nonverbal expression assists in the presentation both of what appears to be a discrepancy and of components that seem to be connected (see next section).

The intent of noting a discrepancy is almost always to challenge. The counselor is not pointing out two or more issues that may or may not be congruent (this would be giving feedback), but rather that there appears, to the counselor, to be a discrepancy. The focus of this response can be client feeling, client thought, and/or client behavior, plus immediacy. This type of response may have multiple focuses because the counselor is pointing out discrepant components.

Examples of Noting a Discrepancy

EXAMPLE 1

#	SPEAKER	VERBATIM RESPONSE	IDENTIFICATION
1.1	CLIENT:	The client is discussing a decision to not move back East with her husband. "What if I am happy being by myself? Yeah, that's scary, that's very scary. What if I end up liking it? What if it feels real good to me and I don't want him back full-time?"	
1.2	COUNSELOR:	"You're talking about being scared, but you're smiling."	■ NOTING A DISCREPANCY ● TO CHALLENGE ▼ CLIENT FEELING and CLIENT BEHAVIOR
1.3	CLIENT:	"I'm smiling, I know. (Client groans and then laughs.) I don't know what that's about. I think it's kind of a nervousness. . . . I think it's hard to acknowledge that."	

EXAMPLE 2

#	SPEAKER	VERBATIM RESPONSE	IDENTIFICATION
2.1	CLIENT:	"I have to get off this fence between teaching and going to night school. As long as I am teaching, it takes so much time and energy that it would be better to just do something that doesn't take so much thought and is on a real schedule."	

#	SPEAKER	VERBATIM RESPONSE	IDENTIFICATION
2.2	COUNSELOR:	"I've heard you mention before that the teaching is something that you really enjoy, and yet you are also talking about the possibility of terminating that."	■ NOTING A DISCREPANCY ● TO CHALLENGE ▼ CLIENT FEELING and CLIENT BEHAVIOR
2.3	CLIENT:	"Well, I think that really what I'd like more of is this—what's called the mentor program, where you are kind of a facilitator between the children and the school and teachers."	

NOTING A CONNECTION

Clients often do not see apparent discrepancies or apparent connections; the counselor, being more objective, can. Egan (1994), as with identifying themes, notes that making connections is part of advanced empathy; "the counselor's job, then, is to help them make the kinds of connections that provide action-oriented insights or perspectives" (p. 183).

Noting a discrepancy and *noting a connection* are similar. They both can be confrontational; each requires the counselor to compare different things that the client has said or done and to present this comparison to the client. The difference is that discrepancies don't seem to go together, connections do.

Paralleling discrepancies, connections can include similarities between

1. What a client is saying or *not* saying and the counselor's perception of what the client is experiencing.
2. What the client is saying and what the counselor heard the client say at another time.
3. What the client is saying in the session and the client's actions outside the session.

As with noting a discrepancy, the intent is to *challenge,* and the focus can be on client feeling, client experience, and/or client behavior and immediacy. As in noting a discrepancy or noting a theme, the counselor can choose to be more explicit ("I see a connection . . ."); more tentative ("It seems that there may be a connection between . . ."); or more implicit (see Example 2).

Examples of Noting a Connection

EXAMPLE 1

#	SPEAKER	VERBATIM RESPONSE	IDENTIFICATION
1.1	CLIENT:	Over the course of several sessions, the client has made numerous references to how poorly he is treated by other people. He talks about his high-stress job and how busy he is.	
1.2	COUNSELOR:	"It seems that there may be a connection between your high stress level and the way you perceive people are treating you."	■ NOTING A CONNECTION ● TO CHALLENGE ▼ CLIENT EXPERIENCE

#	SPEAKER	VERBATIM RESPONSE	IDENTIFICATION
1.3	CLIENT:	(long pause) ". . . Well, maybe. When I'm under stress, I react to people differently . . . and I guess that I may not always hear what they are saying to me. I guess I'd better look at what's going on here."	

EXAMPLE 2

#	SPEAKER	VERBATIM RESPONSE	IDENTIFICATION
2.1	CLIENT:	"Well, I drank too much last night and feel terrible this morning. At least I don't have classes today; I certainly don't feel like doing any homework. The test I took last week, you know the math test, well I flunked that test. I don't know what I'm going to do. That's the second test I've flunked."	
2.2	COUNSELOR:	"I think we need to talk about your drinking and how that affects how you are doing in school."	■ NOTING A CONNECTION ● TO CHALLENGE ▼ CLIENT BEHAVIOR
2.3	CLIENT:	"This really scares me. I'm not sure I want to talk about it . . . but I know I need to."	

⟨13⟩ REFRAMING

*R**eframing* gives the client another view on experiences, feelings, thoughts, behaviors, or the current situation. Often, clients can see the variables of their lives only from their own perspective; the more objective counselor can often see things differently. The counselor, using data from the client, offers an alternative explanation or interpretation of some area of focus, such as

1. An experience: "I wonder if this can be seen as an opportunity to make a change."
2. A feeling: "You say 'anxiety,' but another word may be 'excitement.' "
3. A thought: "You say that you haven't learned anything from this experience, but you have learned how to survive."
4. A behavior: "This feeling may be a signal to avoid the situation."

The counselor may have a very different focus from the client's, because the idea is to offer an alternative view of the issue. Reframing is an invitation to look at something differently. Because it comes from the counselor and is both interpretive and confrontational, it can be offered tentatively. Reframing is intended to *challenge* the client to consider a different perspective. The focus can be on client feeling, client experience, or client behavior and immediacy. Ivey (1994) uses the term *reframing* in conjunction with interpreting:

> Though interpretations may vary in content depending on the theoretical orientation on which they draw, they all have one element in common: the interviewer presents the client with a new frame of reference through which to view the problem or concern and, one hopes, better understand and deal with the situation. (p. 287)

Reframing and playing a hunch are often very close in intent and delivery. Both are designed to present new information, and both depend on the counselor's going beyond what the client is saying. Reframing is suggesting an alternative viewpoint; playing a hunch is sharing the counselor's own interpretation of what may be the case.

Examples of Reframing

EXAMPLE 1

#	SPEAKER	VERBATIM RESPONSE	IDENTIFICATION
1.1	CLIENT:	"I feel very weak admitting how manipulative I am."	
1.2	COUNSELOR:	"Another way of looking at this is that you are being very courageous to want to admit it."	■ REFRAMING ● TO CHALLENGE ▼ CLIENT FEELING

EXAMPLE 2

#	SPEAKER	VERBATIM RESPONSE	IDENTIFICATION
2.1	CLIENT:	"As a child, I learned to shut down my feelings. Now I am very confused about how I feel about everything."	
2.2	COUNSELOR:	"I'd like to suggest your shutting down was a necessary survival response."	■ REFRAMING ● TO CHALLENGE ▼ CLIENT BEHAVIOR

ALLOWING SILENCE

$\mathcal{S}$ ilence is the art of knowing when to be quiet. It is knowing, from attending, when it is more important to let the client process internally rather than verbally. It is believing that it is not the counselor's responsibility either to be talking or to keep the client talking. It is also knowing when to break the silence (and when to allow the client to break the silence) and when to ask the client, for example, "What was going on during that silence?" Silence is verbal silence, which means that nodding, for example, may be appropriate. On the other hand, it may also mean *not* keeping eye contact to give "space."

The counselor needs to think about the timing of being silent as an intentional response—it is not always appropriate. Some client comments need acknowledgment from the counselor. Silence is most useful when the client is engaged in self-analysis, which can be helpful in achieving one goal of counseling, client self-awareness.

Moursund (1993) notes that silence "may be the most useful single intervention available to the therapist" (p. 80). Belkin (1984) agrees:

> Although it is sometimes not recognized as a skillful, facilitative response, silence is one of the most helpful expressions that the counselor can offer to the client. It is particularly useful when the client is engaged in self-analysis, which can be helpful to achieve the ultimate success of the counseling process. (p. 129)

The intent of *allowing silence* generally is to allow clients to *explore,* within themselves, the issue being discussed. The counselor could also intentionally allow silence to *challenge* the client to come up with a response that could grow out of the silence. The focus of silence is always on the client but is not easily differentiated between client feelings, client thought, and client behavior.

Examples of Allowing Silence

EXAMPLE 1

#	SPEAKER	VERBATIM RESPONSE	IDENTIFICATION
1.1	CLIENT:	"I don't know why I get sick . . . maybe it is the stress in my life, the fast pace. . . ."	
1.2	COUNSELOR:	(silence)	■ ALLOWING SILENCE ● TO ACKNOWLEDGE ▼ CLIENT EXPERIENCE
1.3	CLIENT:	"It's kind of nice to just sit here quietly and rest."	

EXAMPLE 2

#	SPEAKER	VERBATIM RESPONSE	IDENTIFICATION
2.1	CLIENT:	"I guess that's where I'm having a hard time with it. . . ." (The client was discussing the difficulty in balancing her job and meeting the needs of her husband.)	
2.2	COUNSELOR:	(silence)	■ ALLOWING SILENCE ● TO EXPLORE ▼ CLIENT EXPERIENCE
2.3	CLIENT:	"I'm not really sure where to go from here. . . , but . . . it seems like I need to make a decision."	

SELF-DISCLOSING

S elf-disclosing is probably the most difficult response to understand, because it requires that the counselor know when and how much information about the counselor might benefit the client. Also, the counselor must be able to keep the focus on the client even though the counselor is sharing personal information. The counselor must be aware of transference and countertransference dynamics and the effect, therapeutically, of self-disclosure on those dynamics. Meier and Davis (1997) suggest:

> Self-disclosing and self-involving statements encourage clients to reciprocate. . . . However, counselors' self-disclosing and self-involving statements should be employed sparingly (to maintain focus on the client) and at a matching level of intensity. . . . It would be inappropriate for a counselor to disclose her or his current feelings of depression to a person seeking career counseling. A more appropriate self-disclosure might involve the counselor's revelation of past feelings of confusion and anxiety surrounding career decisions. (p. 28)

An example of an appropriate self-disclosure that keeps the focus on the client but also establishes a connection with the client is the following: A first-year college student expresses anxiety about her new friends' visiting her and discovering that her family is "really messed up," unlike the families of her friends, which are "perfect." The counselor shares that she felt the same way in her first year of college. The client learns that she is not alone in her feelings, and having connected with the client more personally, the counselor can then share that she learned that her peers in fact did not have perfect families and had the same anxieties. The client then learns to broaden her awareness of her present situation by considering that others may be having similar experiences and that she is not the only person with a "messed-up" family. Thus, her anxiety is lessened.

Kottler and Brown (1996) define self-disclosure as "sharing aspects of the self to deepen the relationship and facilitate movement" (p. 43). Thus, the intent of self-disclosing is often to *acknowledge,* but could be to challenge; the focus is on the counselor, though only temporarily. Should the client want to know more about the counselor's disclosure, the counselor may choose to respond with "How is it for you to hear my experience?" (questioning with the intent to challenge, thus putting the focus back on the client).

Clients may ask the counselor to self-disclose in situations such as the following:

1. A client in a chemical dependency recovery program may ask the counselor if the counselor is recovering. A "counseling" response such as "Is that important for you?" could be viewed as evasive and arrogant. It may be in the therapeutic interest of the client for the counselor to answer and discuss the impact of the answer on the client. It may also help the client to know that the counselor has had similar experiences and has worked through them.

2. A client may ask the counselor how much money the counselor earns (or other personal questions). The counselor may feel it is necessary to be honest in order to

facilitate trust. However, the therapeutic value of the disclosure, let alone the right of privacy for the counselor, may be in question. The counselor can answer in several ways:

a. Honestly.
b. Dishonestly.
c. With a feeling (self-disclosing): "I'm not comfortable answering that question."
d. Using other counseling responses to direct the focus back to the client. This might range from asking for information regarding the client's need to know (for client and counselor understanding) to a confrontation over the discrepancy between the client's issues and the client's focusing on the counselor.

Self-disclosing must always be for the benefit of the client and be designed to keep the focus on the client.

Examples of Self-Disclosing

EXAMPLE 1

#	SPEAKER	VERBATIM RESPONSE	IDENTIFICATION
1.1	CLIENT:	"I feel like an impostor. Everyone in the internship group knows what to do except me. I should never have come to graduate school."	
1.2	COUNSELOR:	"When I started my internship, I felt the same way. I was sure that I was the only person that felt this way. But I learned that everyone felt this way at first."	■ SELF-DISCLOSING ● TO CHALLENGE ▼ CLIENT FEELING

EXAMPLE 2

#	SPEAKER	VERBATIM RESPONSE	IDENTIFICATION
2.1	CLIENT:	"I failed my comprehensive exams, and now I have to take them again. Oh, well, that's the way it goes."	
2.2	COUNSELOR:	"You know, if I had failed my exams, I would be very upset."	■ SELF-DISCLOSING ● TO CHALLENGE ▼ CLIENT FEELING

EXAMPLES OF MULTIPLE
BASIC COUNSELING RESPONSES

Basic counseling responses are generally stronger when stated simply, one at a time. However, combining responses can increase the variety and depth of client responses. The first response can set the stage for the second response. For example, paraphrasing prior to questioning lets the client know that the counselor has been listening and wants the client to respond to questioning relative to the content of the paraphrase. The following examples show how responses can be combined and how the intent and focus of a response can be multiple.

EXAMPLE 1

#	SPEAKER	VERBATIM RESPONSE	IDENTIFICATION
1.1	COUNSELOR:	"I see that you are frowning."	■ GIVING FEEDBACK ● TO ACKNOWLEDGE ▼ CLIENT BEHAVIOR
1.2	COUNSELOR:	"What is going on . . . right now?"	■ QUESTIONING ● TO CHALLENGE ▼ CLIENT FEELING plus IMMEDIACY

EXAMPLE 2

#	SPEAKER	VERBATIM RESPONSE	IDENTIFICATION
		The client was talking about an event that was going to occur on Thursday. She was concerned about what was going to happen and how parents would feel at a school function.	
2.1	COUNSELOR:	"You're talking about what is going to happen on Thursday,	■ GIVING FEEDBACK ● TO ACKNOWLEDGE ▼ CLIENT BEHAVIOR
2.2	COUNSELOR:	but how do you feel now?"	■ QUESTIONING ● TO CHALLENGE ▼ CLIENT FEELING plus IMMEDIACY

EXAMPLE 3

#	SPEAKER	VERBATIM RESPONSE	IDENTIFICATION
		The client is talking about work-related issues.	
3.1	COUNSELOR:	"When you talk about leaving, I just want to share with you that I feel like telling you 'Leave!' . . .	■ SELF-DISCLOSING ● TO CHALLENGE ▼ CLIENT BEHAVIOR
3.2	COUNSELOR:	you sound so miserable.	■ EMPATHIZING ● TO ACKNOWLEDGE ▼ CLIENT FEELING plus IMMEDIACY
3.3	COUNSELOR:	How does it make you feel to hear this?"	■ QUESTIONING ● TO CHALLENGE ▼ CLIENT FEELING plus IMMEDIACY
3.4	CLIENT:	"It makes me feel like, yeah, someone understands. Just turn and walk away. I wish I could do that."	

EXAMPLE 4

#	SPEAKER	VERBATIM RESPONSE	IDENTIFICATION
		The client has been talking about recent tragic deaths and a funeral this week for one of the victims. He said there was closure around these issues. The tense facial and voice expressions and body language don't reflect closure.	
4.1	COUNSELOR:	"I hear you saying that there is closure around the funeral,	■ PARAPHRASING ● TO ACKNOWLEDGE ▼ CLIENT EXPERIENCE
4.2	COUNSELOR:	but your body language and facial expressions don't seem to reflect that.	■ NOTING A DISCREPANCY ● TO CHALLENGE ▼ CLIENT BEHAVIOR
4.3	COUNSELOR:	I hear pain in your voice."	■ EMPATHIZING ● TO ACKNOWLEDGE ▼ CLIENT FEELING
4.4	CLIENT:	"Yes, you are right. I still have some unresolved issues, and I know it is going to take me a while to get over them."	

EXAMPLE 5

#	SPEAKER	VERBATIM RESPONSE	IDENTIFICATION
		The client had become tearful and had a difficult time continuing with the topic. The client was able to further verbalize her feelings and emotions related to the topic.	
5.1	COUNSELOR:	"You've been discussing your emotions and feelings tonight.	■ PARAPHRASING ● TO ACKNOWLEDGE ▼ CLIENT EXPERIENCE
5.2	COUNSELOR:	I wondered how it is for you to share or discuss those feelings with me right now?"	■ QUESTIONING ● TO CHALLENGE ▼ CLIENT EXPERIENCE plus IMMEDIACY
5.3	CLIENT:	"It's fine, I didn't realize that things were going to become as emotional as they did, but that's fine. Whether something like this happens with friends or in a counseling session, there is a reason for whatever is to be happening to happen. It's fine for it to turn out more emotional than I expected it."	

EXTENDED DIALOGUE

The following extended dialogue is a transcript of an entire counseling session to demonstrate how counseling responses, intents, and focuses are identified for each counselor response throughout a session.

#	SPEAKER	VERBATIM RESPONSE	IDENTIFICATION
1	COUNSELOR:	"What would you like to talk about today?"	■ OPENING OR CLOSING ● TO EXPLORE ▼ CLIENT EXPERIENCE
2	CLIENT:	The client begins talking about a visit with her mother. She had gone to her mother's for dinner on Memorial Day. She was upset because her mother had made a comment about never seeing her. "I hate going to see my mom. She always nags me."	
3	COUNSELOR:	"Tell me what you mean when you say your mother 'nags' you."	■ CLARIFYING ● TO EXPLORE ▼ CLIENT EXPERIENCE
4	CLIENT:	"You know, she bugs me about coming to see her. She wanted to know when I was going to get my hair cut. Then she wanted to know if I had been to the cemetery, as there were already some flowers on Dad's grave when she got there." (The client's voice lowers and she twists her ring when she talks about the flowers on her dad's grave.)	
5	COUNSELOR:	"I noticed that the volume of your voice softened as you were talking about visiting the cemetery."	■ GIVING FEEDBACK ● TO ACKNOWLEDGE ▼ CLIENT BEHAVIOR
6	CLIENT:	"Oh, I didn't realize I did that."	
7	COUNSELOR:	(The counselor does not respond.)	■ ALLOWING SILENCE ● TO ACKNOWLEDGE ▼ CLIENT EXPERIENCE

#	SPEAKER	VERBATIM RESPONSE	IDENTIFICATION
8	CLIENT:	(After a few minutes) "Well, yeah, I guess I feel uncomfortable talking about the cemetery."	
9	COUNSELOR:	"What is it about the cemetery that makes you feel uncomfortable?"	■ QUESTIONING ● TO CHALLENGE ▼ CLIENT FEELING
10	CLIENT:	"Oh, I don't know. My mom just likes to nag me. She just asked me because it was one more thing I didn't do that she wanted me to do. Just like wanting me to cut my hair shorter."	
11	COUNSELOR:	"I notice that you did not answer my question about the cemetery."	■ GIVING FEEDBACK ● TO ACKNOWLEDGE ▼ CLIENT BEHAVIOR
12	CLIENT:	"Well, yeah. I really don't like talking about cemeteries. Cemeteries are where dead people are; they are sad places."	
13	COUNSELOR:	"Sad places. . . ."	■ CLARIFYING ● TO EXPLORE ▼ CLIENT EXPERIENCE
14	CLIENT:	"Yeah, sad places. The people who are there are no longer alive. I always see people crying. You never see happy people visiting a cemetery. When I go there, I feel sad."	
15	COUNSELOR:	"You feel sad at the cemetery."	■ EMPATHIZING ● TO ACKNOWLEDGE ▼ CLIENT FEELING
16	CLIENT:	"Yeah, sad. Everybody who visits a cemetery is sad because the person who is buried there is no longer alive. My dad is buried there. That makes me sad because I can no longer see him or talk to him. He understood me a lot more than my mom. I know my mom is right. I should go and visit his grave more often and put flowers on his grave so that people know someone cares for and remembers him. I do care and miss him, and I should put flowers on his grave, but I just don't want to."	

#	SPEAKER	VERBATIM RESPONSE	IDENTIFICATION
17	COUNSELOR:	"I know you say you're sad, but I sense a feeling of anger, too."	■ PLAYING A HUNCH ● TO CHALLENGE ▼ CLIENT FEELING
18	CLIENT:	"Mm . . . Yeah, I guess I am angry. I'm angry because I feel guilty. I feel guilty because I feel like I should visit his grave and put flowers on it regularly but I don't want to. I'm mad at my dad for dying and putting me in this situation. I know I love my dad, but I don't want to feel like I have to go to his grave to show that I loved him. I don't like going to the cemetery because it reminds me that he will never be coming back. I miss my dad."	
19	COUNSELOR:	"My dad died seven years ago, and I still miss him."	■ SELF-DISCLOSING ● TO ACKNOWLEDGE ▼ CLIENT FEELING
20	CLIENT:	"Yeah, I miss my dad. He and I were a lot closer than Mom and I. He understood me. My personality was much more like his than my mother's. You want to know something funny? I still talk to my dad. When I'm troubled, I will talk to him. I'll ask him questions or tell him my problems. And you know, I feel better. I guess that's why I don't like going to the cemetery. It reminds me that he's gone and it makes my imaginary conversations with him seem really stupid."	
21	COUNSELOR:	"I'd like you to imagine that your dad is here right now. Tell him how you feel."	■ DIRECTING ● TO EXPLORE ▼ CLIENT FEELING plus IMMEDIACY
22	CLIENT:	"Dad, I really miss you. Mom doesn't understand me as well as you do. I do love you, but you know me. I don't like cemeteries and never have, ever since I saw Grandma being buried when I was five years old. You understood and never made me go to the cemetery to	

#	SPEAKER	VERBATIM RESPONSE	IDENTIFICATION
		visit Grandma's grave. I'm also mad at you. Mad because you left me and I didn't get to say good-bye. And I'm mad because now I feel guilty because I feel that other people will think I don't love you because I don't come and put flowers on your grave. But I do know that you understand because you know I love you and you know how I feel about cemeteries. I do miss you, Dad, and I love you. Good-bye."	
23	COUNSELOR:	"How do you feel about this exercise I had you do?"	■ QUESTIONING ● TO CHALLENGE ▼ CLIENT FEELING
24	CLIENT:	"You know, I was upset at first, and my first reaction was not to do what you asked. But then I remembered what you said about missing your dad, and I realized that you weren't making fun of me, and the thought crossed my mind that maybe you talked to your dad too. I am really glad I did as you asked. I feel better. I realize now that never saying good-bye was a real issue. I also know my dad does understand, and I really think I can feel a bit more comfortable with visiting my dad in the cemetery. I'll go because I want to, not because I feel obligated to."	
25	COUNSELOR:	"You said good-bye and will now go to the cemetery because you want to, not because you have to."	■ PARAPHRASING ● TO ACKNOWLEDGE ▼ CLIENT EXPERIENCE
26	CLIENT:	"Yeah, I'll do it for me and Dad, not for anyone else."	

PART 3
Exercises

Introduction to Exercises 1–7 for Videocassette and CD-ROM

The seven counseling sessions on the BCR videocassette and CD-ROM are unscripted, actual counseling interactions that have been edited for the CD-ROM and videocassette exercises. All clients volunteered; counselors were selected from graduates of a university-based master's degree program. The sessions are not intended to represent "ideal" counseling interactions, but rather interactions to encourage discussion and critique.

These sessions correspond to Exercises 1–7, respectively, for both the videocassette and CD-ROM. The seven written exercises that follow are for use with the videocassette; if the CD-ROM is used, the exercises are on the CD-ROM itself. Both the worktext exercises and the CD-ROM exercises permit students to work at their own pace. Exercises 1–7 are in a transcript format, allowing users of either the videocassette or the CD-ROM to follow the transcript in written form. The sessions are the same for the videocassette and the CD-ROM. Because Exercises 6 and 7 call for student-created responses, the actual counselor responses are at the end of these exercises in the worktext.

The identification of *responses, intents,* and *focuses* is the primary task in Exercises 1–5. The identification of responses is the easiest task and, in this developmental model, the first. Identifying the focus of each response is usually a new experience for most students, making it somewhat more difficult. By listening to the counselor's language ("You think . . . ," "Your experience has been . . . ," "Right now you feel . . .") , students learn to discern the focus. The most difficult task is identifying the intent. Developmentally, some familiarity and comfort with the responses themselves are necessary before students can name their rationale for the responses they make. Beginning students learn how to be intentional as they start pairing their responses with likely intents. Therefore, after some familiarity with the counseling responses and the focus of the responses, students are expected to discern possible intents of the responses.

In Exercises 1–7, students can compare their identification or creation of responses, intents, and focuses with the suggested responses, intents, and focuses at the end of each exercise. Note that these suggested identifications of responses, intents, and focuses are *suggested*, rather than *correct*. With discussion and discernment, students and instructors may decide that another response, or another identification, is more appropriate.

In Exercise 6, students are given the counseling response, intent, and focus and are asked to create a counselor response, then compare this student-created response to the actual counselor response. In Exercise 7, students identify a specific counseling response, intent, and focus that may be appropriate after the client makes a statement. Then, they create a counselor response that can be compared to the actual response of the counselor. Since student-created responses are requested in Exercises 6 and 7, accuracy and appropriateness can be discerned through supervision.

The clients and counselors portrayed in Exercises 1–7 are diverse in age, gender, and ethnicity. Students are encouraged to answer, in the reflection questions, how age, gender, ethnicity, and disability influence the counseling relationship.

Introduction to the CD-ROM

The accompanying CD-ROM allows the student to observe the seven counseling sessions and complete the respective seven exercises. The system requirements for using the CD-ROM are on the inside cover of this worktext. After inserting the CD-ROM in the computer, click on the BCR icon to start the introduction to the CD-ROM. At any time, the introduction can be skipped by clicking anywhere on the screen. To repeat, click on the screen and then click the Repeat Intro button.

In each session, the counselor is on the left, the client on the right. Each counselor response and each client response is numbered; the numbers correspond to the transcripts in the worktext. When the counselor is responding, the number will be on the left; when the client is talking, the number will be on the right.

This CD-ROM is organized as follows:

1. Click on Select to select sessions 1–7.
2. Click on Observe to see the selected session; the sessions can be observed with or without the response, intent, and focus identified.
3. Click on Exercise to do the selected session exercise.
4. Click on Reflect to answer the reflection question relative to the selected session.
5. Click on File to save completed work to the hard drive or a floppy disk.
6. Click on Help for detailed instructions for observing sessions, completing the exercises, or answering the reflection questions.
7. Click Quit to exit at any time.

The exercises for sessions 1 and 2 call for identification of the counseling response; the exercise for session 3, the focus; the exercise for session 4, the intent; and the exercise for session 5, all three. In these five exercises, the video will stop after each counselor response so the student can identify the response, intent, and/or focus. The exercises for sessions 6 and 7 require keyboarding in student-created responses. The video in 6 and 7 will stop only after certain client responses. Students can then keyboard in their own responses. All exercises have a Compare button so that students can see how their identifications compare to the suggested identifications.

Introduction to Exercises 8–15 for Student Self-Taping

Exercises 8–15 require the student to videotape these sessions with a partner. The exercises are developmental, with each exercise building on the previous one. All exercises include the identification or demonstration of counseling responses, intents, and focuses. As in all counselor training situations, professional supervision is suggested, as these exercises require student-to-student interaction. In Exercises 8 and 9, students practice in a videotaped session, then observe, identify, and reflect. Exercises 10–15 ask the student to demonstrate certain counseling responses, intents, and focuses. Students may initially feel awkward and artificial demonstrating counseling responses. The purpose of these exercises is to become familiar with what a counselor might say. It is expected that with time and further training, students will not only feel more comfortable and confident but will use responses that are therapeutically appropriate.

Introduction to Reflection Questions

Each exercise has questions at the end to facilitate reflection. The questions in Exercises 6 and 7 encourage the student to go back to the created responses and reconsider them after having seen and heard the entire session. A question on the variables affecting the counseling relationship is asked in several exercises to encourage reflection on the significance of these variables.

EXERCISES 1–7 FOR VIDEOCASSETTE WITH TRANSCRIPTS

Exercise 1 for Videocassette: Observe, Identify, Compare, and Reflect

Observe

View session 1 on the BCR videocassette.

Identify

Watch session 1 again, following the transcript below. In the identification column, the counseling response is not shown, but the intent and focus are. Stop the videocassette after each counselor response and fill in a response from one of the 15 basic counseling responses. The first counselor response is filled in as an example. Each counselor response and each client response is numbered on the video and on the transcript.

This exercise calls for a total of 16 counseling response (■) identifications (including the example).

Note: In all videocassette exercises, the identification of responses, intents, and focuses and answers to the reflection questions can be filled in by writing, pages can be removed for typing, or word-processing formats can be created.

Compare

Check suggested response identifications for Exercise 1, following the reflection questions, to compare identified responses.

#	SPEAKER	VERBATIM RESPONSE/TRANSCRIPT	IDENTIFICATION
1.1	COUNSELOR:	"Hi, Steve. Well, thank you for coming today. I just wanted to start by getting a sense of how I can be of help to you."	■ *opening or closing* ● TO EXPLORE ▼ CLIENT EXPERIENCE
1.2	CLIENT	"Oh boy. I'm not quite sure how to put this into words. One of the thoughts that's been running through my head for, I guess for quite a while, that's really getting a lot stronger these days is I've been a student—graduated from high school 11–12 years ago or something like that. I've been in college ever since, and I've been given subtle hints from family and friends and so forth. Just a certain amount of neglect on my part—sort of self-serving. Kind of being very self-absorbed and especially with being a student at this point. I am almost done, at least for quite a while. It's taking a lot more of my focus than it ever has before, and I am becoming frightfully aware of, you know, how much energy I am putting into myself and taking care of my thing and not paying as much attention to my family and my girlfriend. We've got a pretty serious relationship. We've been together quite a while."	
1.3	COUNSELOR:	"Can you describe what you mean by self-absorbed? You mentioned that a couple of times."	■ _____ ● TO EXPLORE ▼ CLIENT EXPERIENCE
1.4	CLIENT:	"Um, just kind of being concerned about my own needs and not necessarily worrying about those of others."	
1.5	COUNSELOR:	"Tell me about those needs."	■ _____ ● TO EXPLORE ▼ CLIENT EXPERIENCE
1.6	CLIENT:	"Um, I was talking with a friend of mine a couple of days ago. He knows both me and my girlfriend fairly well and I was giving him a ride home and he was	

#	SPEAKER	VERBATIM RESPONSE/TRANSCRIPT	IDENTIFICATION
		asking how things were going and I go, 'I feel sorry for her because I'm not even in the room when I'm there—like even when I'm not studying I've got, you know, a hundred other things going through my head or that's what I'm thinking about or things need to get done or this, that, or the other thing.' She's dog-sitting for my parents right now, and I was expressing to my friend that that's a good thing. That she's smart enough to know to not even be around me right now because I am not even a human being when I am in the room."	
1.7	COUNSELOR:	(nod)	■ _____ ● TO ACKNOWLEDGE ▼ CLIENT EXPERIENCE
1.8	COUNSELOR:	"You're not a human being."	■ _____ ● TO CHALLENGE ▼ CLIENT EXPERIENCE
1.9	CLIENT:	"Not—ah—I can't be one to her right now—you know."	
1.10	COUNSELOR:	"Right. Well, I hear you say that you are having a very hard time right now being present because you are very preoccupied with your schoolwork and graduation."	■ _____ ● TO ACKNOWLEDGE ▼ CLIENT EXPERIENCE
1.11	CLIENT:	"Actually graduation isn't even a thought. Just getting the now done—getting that taken care of. You know, it's . . . if it was just something that was coming up right now, it wouldn't really be that big of a concern for me. It's something that I've really noticed and have been told about for quite a while, but now it's like, oh my God—they were right—they've got a point."	
1.12	COUNSELOR:	"It's interesting to me that this seems to be a very upsetting situation. At the same time, I sense that you are smiling and giggling. What's that about?"	■ _____ ● TO CHALLENGE ▼ CLIENT BEHAVIOR

#	SPEAKER	VERBATIM RESPONSE/TRANSCRIPT	IDENTIFICATION
1.13	CLIENT:	"Well, it's almost like a double-edged guilt in a way. On the one hand, I feel like I'm not getting all the schoolwork I need to get done, and on the other hand, I'm not taking care of my relationships in my life."	
1.14	COUNSELOR:	"So, you can't get the job done and you feel guilty—	■ _____ ● TO ACKNOWLEDGE ▼ CLIENT FEELING
1.15	COUNSELOR:	tell me about the guilt."	■ _____ ● TO EXPLORE ▼ CLIENT FEELING
1.16	CLIENT:	"Um, it's kind of different, I guess. On the one hand, I've got kind of an overprotective mother that's always saying 'I want more attention, I want more attention.' It's like mothering is just her thing. I've always been somebody who wanted to be very independent—it's in kind of my nature, I guess. I guess I am coming to the realization I do rely on my parents a lot and I do care, which is—you know—it sounds kind of strange to say. But, you know, and with realizing I do care, I kind of realize how kind of callous I've been and it kind of makes me feel . . ."	
1.17	COUNSELOR:	"Remember I asked you about the guilt and I asked you to tell me about it, and you started talking about the event. Can you just sit with that a minute and focus on your feelings?"	■ _____ ● TO CHALLENGE ▼ CLIENT FEELING
1.18	CLIENT:	"I don't know—it's not an easy thing to do. It's like I almost automatically shut it out. It's like I tune it out, like it's a mechanical property."	
1.19	COUNSELOR:	"It's very hard for you to get in touch with your guilt."	■ _____ ● TO ACKNOWLEDGE ▼ CLIENT FEELING
1.20	CLIENT:	"Yeah."	

#	SPEAKER	VERBATIM RESPONSE/TRANSCRIPT	IDENTIFICATION
1.21	COUNSELOR:	"How are you experiencing the guilt?"	■ _____ ● TO EXPLORE ▼ CLIENT EXPERIENCE
1.22	CLIENT:	"You mean in kind of a schematic way? Boy, it kind of depends on the situation. Like right now, I am feeling it right here (hands on chest). If it's real heavy, then it's down here—my stomach's upset and I can't eat—this, that, or the other thing. Right now it's a real constriction of the chest. I think it's a combination of the stress and guilt and so forth and it kind of focuses here (hand on chest)."	
1.23	COUNSELOR:	"So you experience it right here (hand on chest)?"	■ _____ ● TO ACKNOWLEDGE ▼ CLIENT FEELING
1.24	CLIENT:	"Because I think it's easier to carry that way."	
1.25	COUNSELOR:	"So, we just have a couple of minutes left and I want to make sure that I heard some of the issues correctly today. It sounds like there are some questions about your relationships and the importance of your relationships with your girlfriend and your parents. And at the same time that brings up feelings of guilt for not being able to pay attention the way you'd like to for the people you care about the most."	■ _____ ● TO ACKNOWLEDGE ▼ CLIENT EXPERIENCE
1.26	CLIENT:	"Yeah, that sounds pretty accurate. Yeah, I guess I just haven't really framed it too much other than—that's one of the reasons I had a hard time express-ing it at first."	
1.27	COUNSELOR:	"How's that for you to hear me say that?"	■ _____ ● TO CHALLENGE ▼ CLIENT FEELING plus IMMEDIACY

#	SPEAKER	VERBATIM RESPONSE/TRANSCRIPT	IDENTIFICATION
1.28	CLIENT:	"Um . . . on one hand it's a little frustrating 'cause I have to look at it as a whole, and on the other it's, at least, I can kind of see what's in front of me right now as kind of a temporary thing. You know, and family is always going to be there and that's part of what's going on."	
1.29	COUNSELOR:	"Sounds like this is a good place to stop."	■ _____ ● TO ACKNOWLEDGE ▼ CLIENT EXPERIENCE
1.30	CLIENT:	"Okay."	

Reflect

1. In this session, the female counselor is from South America, the male client from North America. How might these variables influence the counseling relationship?

2. How was the session opened and closed?

3. What are other options for an opening or closing?

Suggested Response Identifications for Exercise 1

1.1   ■ <u>OPENING OR CLOSING</u> ● TO EXPLORE ▼ CLIENT EXPERIENCE

1.3   ■ <u>CLARIFYING</u> ● TO EXPLORE ▼ CLIENT EXPERIENCE

1.5   ■ <u>CLARIFYING</u> ● TO EXPLORE ▼ CLIENT EXPERIENCE

1.7   ■ <u>ATTENDING</u> ● TO ACKNOWLEDGE ▼ CLIENT EXPERIENCE

1.8   ■ <u>PARAPHRASING</u> ● TO CHALLENGE ▼ CLIENT EXPERIENCE

1.10 ■ <u>PARAPHRASING</u> ● TO ACKNOWLEDGE ▼ CLIENT EXPERIENCE

1.12 ■ <u>NOTING A DISCREPANCY</u> ● TO CHALLENGE ▼ CLIENT BEHAVIOR

1.14 ■ <u>PARAPHRASING</u> ● TO ACKNOWLEDGE ▼ CLIENT FEELING

1.15 ■ <u>CLARIFYING</u> ● TO EXPLORE ▼ CLIENT FEELING

1.17 ■ <u>DIRECTING</u> ● TO CHALLENGE ▼ CLIENT FEELING

1.19 ■ <u>EMPATHIZING</u> ● TO ACKNOWLEDGE ▼ CLIENT FEELING

1.21 ■ <u>QUESTIONING</u> ● TO EXPLORE ▼ CLIENT EXPERIENCE

1.23 ■ <u>PARAPHRASING</u> ● TO ACKNOWLEDGE ▼ CLIENT FEELING

1.25 ■ <u>PARAPHRASING</u> ● TO ACKNOWLEDGE ▼ CLIENT EXPERIENCE

1.27 ■ <u>QUESTIONING</u> ● TO CHALLENGE ▼ CLIENT FEELING plus IMMEDIACY

1.29 ■ <u>OPENING OR CLOSING</u> ● TO ACKNOWLEDGE ▼ CLIENT EXPERIENCE

Exercise 2 for Videocassette:
Observe, Identify, Compare, and Reflect

Observe

View session 2 on the BCR videocassette.

Identify

Watch session 2 again, following the transcript below. As in Exercise 1, the counseling response is not shown in the identification column, but the intent and focus are. Stop the videocassette after each counselor response and fill in a counseling response. Each counselor response and each client response is numbered on the video and on the transcript.

This exercise calls for a total of 26 counseling response (■) identifications.

Compare

Check suggested response identifications for Exercise 2, following the reflection questions, to compare identified responses.

#	SPEAKER	VERBATIM RESPONSE/TRANSCRIPT	IDENTIFICATION
2.1	COUNSELOR:	"Okay, Joseph, we are going to meet together for the next 10 weeks and this is our first session, so I am wondering where you'd like to start."	■ _____ ● TO ACKNOWLEDGE ▼ CLIENT EXPERIENCE
2.2	CLIENT:	"Where I'd like to start is probably with the thing that is bothering me the most right now and that's my vision, my loss	

#	SPEAKER	VERBATIM RESPONSE/TRANSCRIPT	IDENTIFICATION
		of vision. Let's see, I was diagnosed with a degenerative eye disease when I was 13. It's called retinitis pigmentosa, degeneration of the rods and cones, which makes me see a very small circle and I need a lot of bright light to see that, and it's really kind of bothering me a lot lately with allergies and the time of season that it is and I am looking at the amount of reading and having to focus and use what vision I have a whole lot these days and I'm just becoming more frustrated and irritated and angry by how much work it is to do just the normal things, you know, that most other people take for granted. And along the same lines I'm having to realize that I am back training with a couple of friends of mine for some triathlons and things, and I've really got to think seriously about how safe it is to be out on a bike by myself competing, you know, possibly in the way of someone else or possibly of doing some harm to myself. So, I'm really thinking seriously about my eyes these days."	
2.3	COUNSELOR:	"What I hear is, with the degeneration of your eyes there's the safety issue and there is the anger and frustration. And I hear that in your voice right now in talking to me."	■ _____ ● TO ACKNOWLEDGE ▼ CLIENT FEELING plus IMMEDIACY
2.4	CLIENT:	"Yeah, that's accurate. And what to do with all that."	
2.5	COUNSELOR:	"What to do with all that, Joseph?"	■ _____ ● TO CHALLENGE ▼ CLIENT BEHAVIOR
2.6	CLIENT:	"I want to be safe for myself and for my significant other and my kids. I don't want anything to happen to me and I also want to challenge myself. I also want to be successful—push a little bit harder—do more, go beyond, you know, what I perceive my limitations are."	

#	SPEAKER	VERBATIM RESPONSE/TRANSCRIPT	IDENTIFICATION
2.7	COUNSELOR:	"It seems real difficult. You want to go beyond what your limitations are, but there's a, I guess almost a constant sense of am I safe."	■ _____ ● TO CHALLENGE ▼ CLIENT FEELING
2.8	CLIENT:	"Yeah, which causes me to hesitate, sometimes, probably in situations that aren't very well lit."	
2.9	COUNSELOR:	"Could you talk about the idea of being unsafe right now?"	■ _____ ● TO EXPLORE ▼ CLIENT FEELING plus IMMEDIACY
2.10	CLIENT:	"Uh, in this particular situation I am very safe. Uh, what is unsafe for me out in the real world? Unfamiliar places that are fairly unlit, that are dark or shaded, become for me like caves. They are, like, well, you know, potentially dangerous. There could be something in the way that I could bump into with my head or trip over. Those types of things. So, those are pretty unsafe. Traveling at 20, 30, or 40 miles per hour on a bike instantaneously becomes unsafe. So, uh, I'm, I find myself—I've been out cycling now twice with a friend—I am holding back on the downhills where I used to be able to just let it go. And I am on the brakes more, and putting on the brakes maybe in order to be safe. So that nothing surprises me and—that it hurts, that I get hurt by."	
2.11	COUNSELOR:	"You talk about you used to be able to tear down the hills and really hang in there with your friends and now you're putting on the brakes and slowing down. You also talk about having a degenerative disease.	■ _____ ● TO ACKNOWLEDGE ▼ CLIENT EXPERIENCE
2.12	COUNSELOR:	I'm wondering, I guess, is it getting worse?"	■ _____ ● TO CHALLENGE ▼ CLIENT EXPERIENCE

#	SPEAKER	VERBATIM RESPONSE/TRANSCRIPT	IDENTIFICATION
2.13	CLIENT:	"Uh, yeah, definitely. I can, I used to be able to notice a difference in my eyesight maybe every 2 to 3 years. Now I am noticing a little bit of a difference maybe once every 6 to 8 months or so. I'll notice that, gosh, I used to be able to see that or I used to be able to not need so much light to do this or that. Yeah."	
2.14	COUNSELOR:	"That must be, I get a sense, really difficult. You are noticing the changes faster now and where is that leading to, I guess it makes me think."	■ _____ ● TO ACKNOWLEDGE ▼ CLIENT FEELING
2.15	CLIENT:	"Um, part of it is—this is my own philosophy—but part of it is that I've been able to, through my own choice of lifestyle, my activity level, I think I've been able to be successful in some ways that have worked to kind of carry me over to be successful in other areas. So, what I'm hesitant to do is give up those areas where I've been able to be successful, you know. Am I still going to be successful in this area even though I am not successful screaming down a hill at 40 or 50 miles an hour?"	
2.16	COUNSELOR:	"And as your vision gets worse . . . it becomes more and more of a problem. Yes?"	■ _____ ● TO EXPLORE ▼ CLIENT EXPERIENCE
2.17	CLIENT:	"Yes."	
2.18	COUNSELOR:	"I'm thinking, am I correct to assume, that the degeneration is leading to you eventually being blind?"	■ _____ ● TO CHALLENGE ▼ CLIENT EXPERIENCE
2.19	CLIENT:	"That's possible, very possible. With retinitis pigmentosa they really don't know—but that's possible."	
2.20	COUNSELOR:	"What's it like for you to hear me say that?"	■ _____ ● TO CHALLENGE ▼ CLIENT FEELING plus IMMEDIACY

#	SPEAKER	VERBATIM RESPONSE/TRANSCRIPT	IDENTIFICATION
2.21	CLIENT:	"Um, I've heard those words for years. It's taken a while to accept those words. In the past 2 years I've progressively been using a cane more. I've just finished a course in Braille, which I resisted for a long time. I resisted a cane as long as possible because I didn't want to be identified as totally blind, which you know I'm not. But I guess with degeneration and slowing down comes an awareness and acceptance of reality that I—that's kind of been forced. But there's the maturity level too—I've got to really think about the long haul."	
2.22	COUNSELOR:	"What's it like for you to be forced to, I guess, see that possibility being more likely?"	■ _____ ● TO CHALLENGE ▼ CLIENT EXPERIENCE
2.23	CLIENT:	"Very resistant, sure, yeah—pretty high resistance. But I don't want to give up my bike. I don't want to necessarily have to depend on, you know, need somebody's help to get down a hallway. I want to be as independent of those types of things for as long as possible, so I've resisted probably more."	
2.24	COUNSELOR:	"What I heard really, sort of sharply, heard was 'somebody's help.'"	■ _____ ● TO ACKNOWLEDGE ▼ CLIENT BEHAVIOR
2.25	CLIENT:	"Uh-huh."	
2.26	COUNSELOR:	"Can you go with that?"	■ _____ ● TO EXPLORE ▼ CLIENT EXPERIENCE
2.27	CLIENT:	"Ah, I think along, along with becoming less independent for example on a, on a bike or mobility wise, I think, becoming less independent sometimes means, may mean, more dependent, more need to require the assistance of other people to do things."	

#	SPEAKER	VERBATIM RESPONSE/TRANSCRIPT	IDENTIFICATION
2.28	COUNSELOR:	"You know, even as you talk about the idea of becoming more dependent, I see almost within a sense of, that you are almost staying independent. The idea of working with a cane, learning Braille, that there's a very big independence throughout all of this that I hear. Does that sort of fit with you?"	■ _____ ● TO CHALLENGE ▼ CLIENT EXPERIENCE
2.29	CLIENT:	"Yes, yeah. I'd like to maintain as much independence as possible."	
2.30	COUNSELOR:	(silence)	■ _____ ● TO ACKNOWLEDGE ▼ CLIENT EXPERIENCE
2.31	CLIENT:	"I guess I'm resistant to, to need anybody else."	
2.32	COUNSELOR:	"I heard your voice change right there. When you said 'I am resistant to need,' I heard your voice get softer, quieter.	■ _____ ● TO ACKNOWLEDGE ▼ CLIENT BEHAVIOR
2.33	COUNSELOR:	What's going on for you now?"	■ _____ ● TO CHALLENGE ▼ CLIENT EXPERIENCE plus IMMEDIACY
2.34	CLIENT:	"Ah, there's a part of me that doesn't want to need anybody's help. There's a part of me that doesn't want to be dependent. There's a part of me that doesn't want to give up that independence and I'm afraid—I am afraid of losing myself in that need for dependence."	
2.35	COUNSELOR:	"As your vision gets worse, you need help from more people, you need more help from people rather, and as you need, as you receive more help from more people, you lose yourself, you lose some of yourself."	■ _____ ● TO ACKNOWLEDGE ▼ CLIENT EXPERIENCE
2.36	CLIENT:	"Yeah, yeah. So I try to hang onto or maintain those things or do those things to foster the kind of independence that—or as much of	

#	SPEAKER	VERBATIM RESPONSE/TRANSCRIPT	IDENTIFICATION
		the independence that I have known, you know, in the past. I want to try to hang onto that."	
2.37	COUNSELOR:	"Yeah, yeah, that's almost a theme that I get throughout everything that we've talked about. That hanging onto the independence. Almost fighting very hard to hang on to that independence."	■ _____ ● TO CHALLENGE ▼ CLIENT EXPERIENCE
2.38	CLIENT:	"Yeah."	
2.39	COUNSELOR:	"We're going to finish in about a minute. We've been together for about 10–15 minutes.	■ _____ ● TO ACKNOWLEDGE ▼ CLIENT EXPERIENCE
2.40	COUNSELOR:	Could you tell me what was important, what was helpful today?"	■ _____ ● TO EXPLORE ▼ CLIENT EXPERIENCE
2.41	CLIENT:	"Um, I think it was real helpful for me to just be able to talk about the most important issue directly confronting me at this moment in time. Right now, today."	
2.42	COUNSELOR:	"And could you name that?"	■ _____ ● TO CHALLENGE ▼ CLIENT EXPERIENCE
2.43	CLIENT:	"The loss of, the potential loss of my vision."	
2.44	COUNSELOR:	"Okay, yeah. That's a hard thing. It must be—it's I don't know—	■ _____ ● TO ACKNOWLEDGE ▼ CLIENT FEELING
2.45	COUNSELOR:	it's actually difficult for me to hear you say it even, you know.	■ _____ ● TO ACKNOWLEDGE ▼ CLIENT FEELING
2.46	COUNSELOR:	We're going to finish now, and I will see you next week and we can keep working on this. Okay?"	■ _____ ● TO ACKNOWLEDGE ▼ CLIENT EXPERIENCE
2.47	CLIENT:	"Okay."	
2.48	COUNSELOR:	"Thank you."	
2.49	CLIENT:	"Thank you."	

Reflect

1. In this session, the counselor is a person with sight, the client is a person with limited vision. How might this variable influence the counseling relationship?

2. Identify examples of the counselor's genuineness and respect, and discuss how they may have influenced the counseling session.

Suggested Response Identifications for Exercise 2

2.1   ■ OPENING OR CLOSING ● TO ACKNOWLEDGE ▼ CLIENT EXPERIENCE

2.3   ■ PARAPHRASING ● TO ACKNOWLEDGE ▼ CLIENT FEELING plus IMMEDIACY

2.5   ■ QUESTIONING ● TO CHALLENGE ▼ CLIENT BEHAVIOR

2.7   ■ PLAYING A HUNCH ● TO CHALLENGE ▼ CLIENT FEELING

2.9   ■ CLARIFYING ● TO EXPLORE ▼ CLIENT FEELING plus IMMEDIACY

2.11 ■ PARAPHRASING ● TO ACKNOWLEDGE ▼ CLIENT EXPERIENCE

2.12 ■ QUESTIONING ● TO CHALLENGE ▼ CLIENT EXPERIENCE

2.14 ■ EMPATHIZING ● TO ACKNOWLEDGE ▼ CLIENT FEELING

2.16 ■ QUESTIONING ● TO EXPLORE ▼ CLIENT EXPERIENCE

2.18 ■ QUESTIONING ● TO CHALLENGE ▼ CLIENT EXPERIENCE

2.20 ■ QUESTIONING ● TO CHALLENGE ▼ CLIENT FEELING plus IMMEDIACY

2.22 ■ QUESTIONING ● TO CHALLENGE ▼ CLIENT EXPERIENCE

2.24 ■ GIVING FEEDBACK ● TO ACKNOWLEDGE ▼ CLIENT BEHAVIOR

2.26 ■ CLARIFYING ● TO EXPLORE ▼ CLIENT EXPERIENCE

2.28 ■ REFRAMING ● TO CHALLENGE ▼ CLIENT EXPERIENCE

2.30 ■ ALLOWING SILENCE ● TO ACKNOWLEDGE ▼ CLIENT EXPERIENCE

2.32   ■ <u>GIVING FEEDBACK</u> ● TO ACKNOWLEDGE ▼ CLIENT BEHAVIOR

2.33   ■ <u>QUESTIONING</u> ● TO CHALLENGE ▼ CLIENT EXPERIENCE plus IMMEDIACY

2.35   ■ <u>PARAPHRASING</u> ● TO ACKNOWLEDGE ▼ CLIENT EXPERIENCE

2.37   ■ <u>NOTING A THEME</u> ● TO CHALLENGE ▼ CLIENT EXPERIENCE

2.39   ■ <u>OPENING OR CLOSING</u> ● TO ACKNOWLEDGE ▼ CLIENT EXPERIENCE

2.40   ■ <u>QUESTIONING</u> ● TO EXPLORE ▼ CLIENT EXPERIENCE

2.42   ■ <u>QUESTIONING</u> ● TO CHALLENGE ▼ CLIENT EXPERIENCE

2.44   ■ <u>EMPATHIZING</u> ● TO ACKNOWLEDGE ▼ CLIENT FEELING

2.45   ■ <u>SELF-DISCLOSING</u> ● TO ACKNOWLEDGE ▼ CLIENT FEELING

2.46   ■ <u>OPENING OR CLOSING</u> ● TO ACKNOWLEDGE ▼ CLIENT EXPERIENCE

Exercise 3 for Videocassette: Observe, Identify, Compare, and Reflect

Observe

View session 3 on the BCR videocassette.

Identify

Watch session 3 again, following the transcript below. In the identification column, the counseling response and the intent are shown, but not the focus. Stop the videocassette after each counselor response and fill in a focus from the one of the four focuses, plus the additional focus of immediacy if appropriate. Each counselor response and each client response is numbered on the video and on the transcript.

This exercise calls for a total of 23 focus (▼) identifications.

Compare

Check suggested focus identifications for Exercise 3, following the reflection questions, to compare identified focuses.

#	SPEAKER	VERBATIM RESPONSE/TRANSCRIPT	IDENTIFICATION
3.1	COUNSELOR:	"Hi, Paul, you signed up to see me today?"	■ OPENING OR CLOSING ● TO ACKNOWLEDGE ▼＿＿＿＿＿＿

#	SPEAKER	VERBATIM RESPONSE/TRANSCRIPT	IDENTIFICATION
3.2	CLIENT:	"My PE teacher has been criticizing our class and she's been making me very sad, like feeling not too well about myself—making me feel like I—I am not very good and I, she like—it's like she hates—not really hates, but she's making me feel real small, I guess. Like real—not—like real—like she doesn't like us and she doesn't want us to do much. And she's been kind of really making me feel real small. I feel pretty sad about that—that she, it's like she doesn't really like us and our class, she's been criticizing it—she said like we're the worst class for doing team stuff."	
3.3	COUNSELOR:	"I notice you said 'we' and think you were talking about your class and then you also said 'I.' "	■ GIVING FEEDBACK ● TO ACKNOWLEDGE ▼ _____
3.4	CLIENT:	"Uh-huh—like every one of us. She—we feel the same way, I think."	
3.5	COUNSELOR:	"Also, when you were talking—you said 'It makes me feel small'—you sort of move forward."	■ GIVING FEEDBACK ● TO ACKNOWLEDGE ▼ _____
3.6	CLIENT:	"Yeah—like I don't really have much power against it and she doesn't let us— she says she wouldn't let us do much so that we don't get to do much. She makes us feel like we're real bad."	
3.7	COUNSELOR:	"Uh-huh. Can you take a specific incident that you remember?"	■ CLARIFYING ● TO EXPLORE ▼ _____
3.8	CLIENT:	"Well, there's this one time—it was on the last day we were seeing her—we were sitting down in a circle and discussing this one problem that we had on a day we were playing a game and we were like asking her how come she couldn't run it and stuff. How come she couldn't help us with it, and she said that like we were the worst class on	

#	SPEAKER	VERBATIM RESPONSE/TRANSCRIPT	IDENTIFICATION
		doing it and like need to shape up and really try and do it and she—she was a part—she played that game with us, but she didn't help us run it and I think she should of. Then she said, like, started talking to us and said we were the worst class for doing team stuff."	
3.9	COUNSELOR:	"So let me hear if I understood you. You said that you had a discussion as a class and then you gave her some information that you wanted her to help your team a little bit and then you played the game."	■ PARAPHRASING ● TO ACKNOWLEDGE ▼ _____
3.10	CLIENT:	"Well, yeah. We kinda played it and she kinda mixed me real up because she said I'm just stating a simple fact and later on she'd tell us it was her opinion. So she was making me like real confused and small."	
3.11	COUNSELOR:	"Uh-huh. You've used 'feeling small' several times when you've talked about what is going on in PE.	■ GIVING FEEDBACK ● TO ACKNOWLEDGE ▼ _____
3.12	COUNSELOR:	Can you be specific about the feeling small?"	■ CLARIFYING ● TO EXPLORE ▼ _____
3.13	CLIENT:	"Well, like we can't do anything to help this, and like small as in like if she was like real powerful. She made it seem like she was real powerful and we—and we—couldn't really do much. And so we're kind of small in power and stuff and small in doing stuff."	
3.14	COUNSELOR:	"So, like if we were just to look at how you're feeling in the class, I have a feeling that the teacher is up here—you're using the word 'powerful'—and then I feel like Paul's down here—real small."	■ PLAYING A HUNCH ● TO CHALLENGE ▼ _____
3.15	CLIENT:	"Yeah, we can't do much and she really stated it and made it real mean."	

#	SPEAKER	VERBATIM RESPONSE/TRANSCRIPT	IDENTIFICATION
3.16	COUNSELOR:	"So when you two are back here and she has the power and she's stating things that you're hearing and feeling that she's being mean."	■ PARAPHRASING ● TO ACKNOWLEDGE ▼ _____
3.17	CLIENT:	"Uh-huh."	
3.18	COUNSELOR:	"How does that affect you?"	■ QUESTIONING ● TO CHALLENGE ▼ _____
3.19	CLIENT:	"It makes me like, kind of like, it makes me feel like—kind of like that she doesn't want us to do stuff. And one of our friends stated something that most of us can, like, he can do many things in physical activities and she just kept on stating that we could not do it. And made us real angry at her, I guess and also small."	
3.20	COUNSELOR:	"You know when I sort of put my hands like this after listening to you. It seems like you, even though you had a discussion and your friend was trying to talk to the teacher, it seems like there isn't much communication happening there."	■ PLAYING A HUNCH ● TO CHALLENGE ▼ _____
3.21	CLIENT:	"No, 'cause she just kept on saying that it doesn't work out—when it does, usually. When we played the game called car park it was fine."	
3.22	COUNSELOR:	"When you're not able to communicate with someone, how does that—how's that for you? When you can't communicate with someone."	■ QUESTIONING ● TO CHALLENGE ▼ _____
3.23	CLIENT:	"It makes me frustrated. Sometimes it makes me scared. I'd really like to do something about it, but sometimes I just feel like I shouldn't do it—cause I might something—like I might be in trouble or something."	

#	SPEAKER	VERBATIM RESPONSE/TRANSCRIPT	IDENTIFICATION
3.24	COUNSELOR:	"So you feel scared and frustrated and also maybe wanting to take action?"	■ PARAPHRASING ● TO ACKNOWLEDGE ▼ _____
3.25	CLIENT:	"Yeah. Like, I'd really like to do something about it. But she just makes it, she just sounds so mean sometimes. She kind of says it really calmly but then she just like starts playing something. And like my guess is that she's trying to have us forget it and the way she says it does not make me forget it, at least. And so she's like being real, I think, bad communicating to us. She won't let us communicate to her, and we, it's like we're powerless over her. And we have to do what she does. So . . ."	
3.26	COUNSELOR:	"I know one of the things that I am seeing is that by signing up to come to see me is that part of taking action on your part."	■ REFRAMING ● TO CHALLENGE ▼ _____
3.27	CLIENT:	"Um, yeah, I think so."	
3.28	COUNSELOR:	"How so?"	■ QUESTIONING ● TO CHALLENGE ▼ _____
3.29	CLIENT:	"Well, maybe that somebody else could help me with it. Somebody older, somebody that could like maybe talk to her to see if she could stop it instead of us."	
3.30	COUNSELOR:	"If she could stop."	■ CLARIFYING ● TO EXPLORE ▼ _____
3.31	CLIENT:	"If she could like stop her saying we were bad and stuff and let us do more activities."	
3.32	COUNSELOR:	"So, are there perhaps three issues? One is being able to talk to her, one is the addressing the stopping the putting down, and the other is the type of activities done in PE? Is that . . ."	■ PARAPHRASING ● TO ACKNOWLEDGE ▼ _____

#	SPEAKER	VERBATIM RESPONSE/TRANSCRIPT	IDENTIFICATION
3.33	CLIENT:	"She won't let us do many team things."	
3.34	COUNSELOR:	"Okay—so are there three things that are of concern?"	■ PARAPHRASING ● TO ACKNOWLEDGE ▼ _____
3.35	CLIENT:	"Uh-huh."	
3.36	COUNSELOR:	"Okay. We only have a couple of minutes left. What would you like to . . . you know, we've talked about what the issues are—concerns for you. Where—where would you like to go with this?"	■ QUESTIONING ● TO CHALLENGE ▼ _____
3.37	CLIENT:	"I'm not really sure. Maybe we could like, we could talk about it, maybe, well we could like talk about it to her after this."	
3.38	COUNSELOR:	"Uh-huh. So one of the ideas is maybe . . . you said the word 'we,' who was in the 'we' part?"	■ QUESTIONING ● TO EXPLORE ▼ _____
3.39	CLIENT:	"Me and you."	
3.40	COUNSELOR:	"Okay, so maybe you and I could talk with her."	■ PARAPHRASING ● TO ACKNOWLEDGE ▼ _____
3.41	CLIENT:	"Uh-huh."	
3.42	COUNSELOR:	"Okay. What about if we meet tomorrow and take some time to explore your idea of meeting and what that would mean? And sometimes it's helpful to talk ahead of time how you think that might go."	■ DIRECTING ● TO CHALLENGE ▼ _____
3.43	CLIENT:	"Okay, we can talk tomorrow."	
3.44	COUNSELOR:	"Okay, sounds good. Okay. Thank you."	■ OPENING OR CLOSING ● TO ACKNOWLEDGE ▼ _____

Reflect

1. In this session, the client is of elementary-school age. How might this variable influence how the counselor responds to the client?

2. The counselor is going to see this student again. Discuss some ideas or strategies for the next session.

Suggested Focus Identifications for Exercise 3

3.1   ■ OPENING OR CLOSING ● TO ACKNOWLEDGE ▼ <u>CLIENT EXPERIENCE</u>

3.3   ■ GIVING FEEDBACK ● TO ACKNOWLEDGE ▼ <u>CLIENT BEHAVIOR</u>

3.5   ■ GIVING FEEDBACK ● TO ACKNOWLEDGE ▼ <u>CLIENT BEHAVIOR</u>

3.7   ■ CLARIFYING ● TO EXPLORE ▼ <u>CLIENT EXPERIENCE</u>

3.9   ■ PARAPHRASING ● TO ACKNOWLEDGE ▼ <u>CLIENT EXPERIENCE</u>

3.11 ■ GIVING FEEDBACK ● TO ACKNOWLEDGE ▼ <u>CLIENT BEHAVIOR</u>

3.12 ■ CLARIFYING ● TO EXPLORE ▼ <u>CLIENT FEELING</u>

3.14 ■ PLAYING A HUNCH ● TO CHALLENGE ▼ <u>CLIENT FEELING</u>

3.16 ■ PARAPHRASING ● TO ACKNOWLEDGE ▼ <u>CLIENT EXPERIENCE</u>

3.18 ■ QUESTIONING ● TO CHALLENGE ▼ <u>CLIENT EXPERIENCE</u>

3.20 ■ PLAYING A HUNCH ● TO CHALLENGE ▼ <u>CLIENT EXPERIENCE</u>

3.22 ■ QUESTIONING ● TO CHALLENGE ▼ <u>CLIENT EXPERIENCE</u>

3.24 ■ PARAPHRASING ● TO ACKNOWLEDGE ▼ <u>CLIENT FEELING</u>

3.26 ■ REFRAMING ● TO CHALLENGE ▼ <u>CLIENT BEHAVIOR</u>

3.28 ■ QUESTIONING ● TO CHALLENGE ▼ <u>CLIENT THOUGHT</u>

3.30 ■ CLARIFYING ● TO EXPLORE ▼ <u>CLIENT THOUGHT</u>

3.32 ■ PARAPHRASING ● TO ACKNOWLEDGE ▼ <u>CLIENT EXPERIENCE</u>

3.34 ■ PARAPHRASING ● TO ACKNOWLEDGE ▼ <u>CLIENT EXPERIENCE</u>

3.36 ■ QUESTIONING ● TO CHALLENGE ▼ <u>CLIENT EXPERIENCE</u>

3.38 ■ QUESTIONING ● TO EXPLORE ▼ <u>CLIENT THOUGHT</u>

3.40 ■ PARAPHRASING ● TO ACKNOWLEDGE ▼ <u>CLIENT BEHAVIOR</u>

3.42 ■ DIRECTING ● TO CHALLENGE ▼ <u>CLIENT BEHAVIOR</u>

3.44 ■ OPENING OR CLOSING ● TO ACKNOWLEDGE ▼ <u>CLIENT EXPERIENCE</u>

Exercise 4 for Videocassette: Observe, Identify, Compare, and Reflect

Observe

View session 4 on the BCR videocassette.

Identify

Watch session 4 again, following the transcript below. In the identification column, the intent is not shown, but the counseling response and focus are. Stop the videocassette after each counselor response and fill in one of the three intents.

This exercise calls for a total of 34 intent (●) identifications.

Compare

Check suggested intent identifications for Exercise 4, following the reflection questions, to compare identified intents.

#	SPEAKER	VERBATIM RESPONSE/TRANSCRIPT	IDENTIFICATION
4.1	COUNSELOR:	"Paul, yesterday you and I agreed that we'd meet again today."	■ OPENING OR CLOSING ● _____ ▼ CLIENT EXPERIENCE
4.2	CLIENT:	"Uh-huh."	
4.3	COUNSELOR:	"Have you been thinking about what we talked about yesterday?"	■ QUESTIONING ● _____ ▼ CLIENT THOUGHT

#	SPEAKER	VERBATIM RESPONSE/TRANSCRIPT	IDENTIFICATION
4.4	CLIENT:	"Yeah, and I think I'd like to go and talk to my PE teacher and see if you can help."	
4.5	COUNSELOR:	"Let's take that sort of one step at a time. What is—what information or what would you like to tell your teacher?"	■ DIRECTING ● _____ ▼ CLIENT BEHAVIOR
4.6	CLIENT:	"Well , I'd like to tell her stop making our class—stop telling our class we're real bad. And maybe, like, to tell her if you don't have something good to say don't say it at all. Just stop it."	
4.7	COUNSELOR:	"One of the things that I find really helpful is if when I am talking to someone I use 'I' statements. Looking again at someone putting you down—	■ SELF-DISCLOSING ● _____ ▼ CLIENT BEHAVIOR
4.8	COUNSELOR:	how could you tell your PE teacher that in an 'I' statement?"	■ QUESTIONING ● _____ ▼ CLIENT BEHAVIOR
4.9	CLIENT:	"Um, I would like you to stop putting me down and stop doing it because I don't like it and it makes me feel real bad."	
4.10	COUNSELOR:	"When you just said that, how did that feel to say that?"	■ QUESTIONING ● _____ ▼ CLIENT FEELING plus IMMEDIACY
4.11	CLIENT:	(Sigh) "It felt pretty good to say it."	
4.12	COUNSELOR:	"The second part of what you said at the beginning when you came in was, 'We would go to talk to my PE teacher.' Can you expand on that?"	■ CLARIFYING ● _____ ▼ CLIENT BEHAVIOR
4.13	CLIENT:	"Well, I'd like to, yeah, I think I could, like we could go and talk and see if we could help her stop talking that way to us. See if she would stop."	

#	SPEAKER	VERBATIM RESPONSE/TRANSCRIPT	IDENTIFICATION
4.14	COUNSELOR:	"I heard you say two different things. I heard you say 'we could' and 'I could.'	■ GIVING FEEDBACK ● _____ ▼ CLIENT BEHAVIOR
4.15	COUNSELOR:	Are those two different things? 'I could' . . . 'we could'?"	■ QUESTIONING ● _____ ▼ CLIENT THOUGHT
4.16	CLIENT:	"No, not really, 'cause I would try and do it and I was hoping me and you could do it. So, they are kind of in the same way I would like to stop her."	
4.17	COUNSELOR:	"So, when you told me one of the things you'd like to share with her was put in an 'I' statement—sounds like you are ready to talk to her."	■ PLAYING A HUNCH ● _____ ▼ CLIENT BEHAVIOR
4.18	CLIENT:	(nods)	
4.19	COUNSELOR:	"And then I would be coming along to do what?"	■ QUESTIONING ● _____ ▼ CLIENT THOUGHT
4.20	CLIENT:	"To help me explain to her, 'cause I don't really feel too happy around her and I might need a little help explaining it to her. 'Cause I'm kinda just a kid. You're bigger and you can probably tell her."	
4.21	COUNSELOR:	"Okay, when you said 'I'm just kinda a kid,' does that get into the teacher is here and you're right there?"	■ PLAYING A HUNCH ● _____ ▼ CLIENT EXPERIENCE
4.22	CLIENT:	"Uh-huh."	
4.23	COUNSELOR:	"And you're feeling that it is hard to communicate straight across?"	■ PARAPHRASING ● _____ ▼ CLIENT FEELING
4.24	CLIENT:	"Uh-huh."	
4.25	COUNSELOR:	"You're a student and I am a counselor, sometimes seen as a teacher. How do you feel it is to be here to talk to me right now?"	■ QUESTIONING ● _____ ▼ CLIENT FEELING plus IMMEDIACY

#	SPEAKER	VERBATIM RESPONSE/TRANSCRIPT	IDENTIFICATION
4.26	CLIENT:	"I feel real good because I think I am going to get some help on stopping my teacher—the PE teacher—from telling us what she's thinking and hoping that she'll stop."	
4.27	COUNSELOR:	"Paul, sometimes when students ask if I can go with them to help talk with a teacher, I am able to do that.	■ SELF-DISCLOSING ● _____ ▼ CLIENT BEHAVIOR
4.28	COUNSELOR:	One of the things that we need to decide on is how we are going to do that.	■ DIRECTING ● _____ ▼ CLIENT BEHAVIOR
4.29	COUNSELOR:	First of all, I think we need to, one of us needs to let the teacher know that we would like to meet with them and see if the three of us can have a meeting. Then, second part is if that's convenient and if they are willing to meet us, is who is going to be talking, to express what is going on."	■ DIRECTING ● _____ ▼ CLIENT THOUGHT
4.30	CLIENT:	"Well, I think I might be able to tell, ask her if we can have a meeting sometime. Next time I see her in PE I might be able to arrange a meeting."	
4.31	COUNSELOR:	"Uh-huh. How would you go about doing that?"	■ QUESTIONING ● _____ ▼ CLIENT BEHAVIOR
4.32	CLIENT:	"Well, probably, either when I first come in, I'll, I guess, I will ask her if we can have, if we can talk at, like, whichever date we would arrange. See if she would come to it, or if she would not be able to go or something and see if I could get her to meet with us and then I guess then, hopefully, she would come and we could talk about it with her."	
4.33	COUNSELOR:	"Okay. And who'd do the talking? Giving the examples and expressing the concerns?"	■ QUESTIONING ● _____ ▼ CLIENT BEHAVIOR

#	SPEAKER	VERBATIM RESPONSE/TRANSCRIPT	IDENTIFICATION
4.34	CLIENT:	"I guess maybe I would and then if I wanted you to maybe help me talk. That's one of the reasons I came here— to see if you could help me explain it to her."	
4.35	COUNSELOR:	"Can you give me an example of what I might be doing to help?"	■ QUESTIONING ● _____ ▼ CLIENT THOUGHT
4.36	CLIENT:	"Well, like you might be able to tell her what she really needs to do and stuff and see if you can stop her doing it."	
4.37	COUNSELOR:	"So you are the person that is going to maybe give her the example and make the request: Can you stop?"	■ PARAPHRASING ● _____ ▼ CLIENT BEHAVIOR
4.38	CLIENT:	"Then hopefully she will."	
4.39	COUNSELOR:	"So, it sounds like it means that we might need to get together again to see if it does stop."	■ PLAYING A HUNCH ● _____ ▼ CLIENT EXPERIENCE
4.40	CLIENT:	"Uh-huh."	
4.41	COUNSELOR:	"All right. You have a smile on your face right now, don't you?	■ GIVING FEEDBACK ● _____ ▼ CLIENT BEHAVIOR plus IMMEDIACY
4.42	COUNSELOR:	What's the smile for?"	■ QUESTIONING ● _____ ▼ CLIENT BEHAVIOR
4.43	CLIENT:	" 'Cause I'm real happy that she's prob—hopefully going to stop and we're gonna—we can have her stop and then it's going to be fine and we can have fun and play team games again."	
4.44	COUNSELOR:	"So, you're feeling some confidence in the plan that you've come up with and you feel this plan is a little different enough than the last time you tried to talk with her as a group?"	■ PARAPHRASING ● _____ ▼ CLIENT FEELING
4.45	CLIENT:	(nods)	

#	SPEAKER	VERBATIM RESPONSE/TRANSCRIPT	IDENTIFICATION
4.46	COUNSELOR:	"What might the differences be, talking to her individually versus a class talking to her?"	■ QUESTIONING ● _____ ▼ CLIENT BEHAVIOR
4.47	CLIENT:	"Well, I am going to have someone older with me and I'm gonna probably have a better plan. So, it's more likely it would happen 'cause we didn't really have much of a plan when we tried to have her to stop when we were in PE. So, now I have a plan and now I've got somebody big with me and I can—it's more likely to happen."	
4.48	COUNSELOR:	"Okay. How does it feel to say 'It's more likely to happen'?"	■ QUESTIONING ● _____ ▼ CLIENT FEELING
4.49	CLIENT:	"Feels real good. That I'm working out one of my problems. So I can maybe work out a lot more."	
4.50	COUNSELOR:	"Sounds like you're saying that you learned a lesson, or that there's a lesson here?"	■ PARAPHRASING ● _____ ▼ CLIENT EXPERIENCE
4.51	CLIENT:	"Yeah, I guess—kind of."	
4.52	COUNSELOR:	"Is there something you've learned about taking the time to think about a different plan?"	■ QUESTIONING ● _____ ▼ CLIENT EXPERIENCE
4.53	CLIENT:	"Sort of."	
4.54	COUNSELOR:	"What might that be?"	■ QUESTIONING ● _____ ▼ CLIENT EXPERIENCE
4.55	CLIENT:	"Probably be to—probably be to see if you could stop it and devise a plan."	
4.56	COUNSELOR:	"By you—can you say that again with just talking about yourself saying 'I'?"	■ DIRECTING ● _____ ▼ CLIENT BEHAVIOR
4.57	CLIENT:	"To see—to see if I could make a plan and try to see if it will work. This lesson will probably help me to make more plans in the future."	

#	SPEAKER	VERBATIM RESPONSE/TRANSCRIPT	IDENTIFICATION
4.58	COUNSELOR:	"Okay. So before you go, let me make sure we are both hearing the same thing. That you're going to be in touch with the PE teacher."	■ PARAPHRASING ● _____ ▼ CLIENT BEHAVIOR
4.59	CLIENT:	(nods)	
4.60	COUNSELOR:	"Arrange for a time that is convenient for the three of us to sit down. And then we'll sit down and meet and then maybe you can stop by sometime to check in with me to let me know how things went."	■ PARAPHRASING ● _____ ▼ CLIENT EXPERIENCE
4.61	CLIENT:	"Okay."	
4.62	COUNSELOR:	"Okay, all right, thank you."	■ OPENING OR CLOSING ● _____ ▼ CLIENT EXPERIENCE

Reflect

1. How were the ideas or strategies named in Exercise 3, question 2, played out in this second session?

2. Discuss how counseling may be different in a school setting from in a counseling agency or private practice.

Suggested Intent Identifications for Exercise 4

4.1   ■ OPENING OR CLOSING ● TO ACKNOWLEDGE ▼ CLIENT EXPERIENCE

4.3   ■ QUESTIONING ● TO CHALLENGE ▼ CLIENT THOUGHT

4.5   ■ DIRECTING ● TO CHALLENGE ▼ CLIENT BEHAVIOR

4.7   ■ SELF-DISCLOSING ● TO CHALLENGE ▼ CLIENT BEHAVIOR

4.8   ■ QUESTIONING ● TO CHALLENGE ▼ CLIENT BEHAVIOR

4.10   ■ QUESTIONING ● TO CHALLENGE ▼ CLIENT FEELING plus IMMEDIACY

4.12   ■ CLARIFYING ● TO EXPLORE ▼ CLIENT BEHAVIOR

4.14   ■ GIVING FEEDBACK ● TO ACKNOWLEDGE ▼ CLIENT BEHAVIOR

4.15   ■ QUESTIONING ● TO CHALLENGE ▼ CLIENT THOUGHT

4.17   ■ PLAYING A HUNCH ● TO CHALLENGE ▼ CLIENT BEHAVIOR

4.19   ■ QUESTIONING ● TO EXPLORE ▼ CLIENT THOUGHT

4.21   ■ PLAYING A HUNCH ● TO CHALLENGE ▼ CLIENT EXPERIENCE

4.23   ■ PARAPHRASING ● TO ACKNOWLEDGE ▼ CLIENT FEELING

4.25   ■ QUESTIONING ● TO CHALLENGE ▼ CLIENT FEELING plus IMMEDIACY

4.27   ■ SELF-DISCLOSING ● TO CHALLENGE ▼ CLIENT BEHAVIOR

4.28   ■ DIRECTING ● TO CHALLENGE ▼ CLIENT BEHAVIOR

4.29   ■ DIRECTING ● TO CHALLENGE ▼ CLIENT THOUGHT

4.31   ■ QUESTIONING ● TO CHALLENGE ▼ CLIENT BEHAVIOR

4.33   ■ QUESTIONING ● TO CHALLENGE ▼ CLIENT/BEHAVIOR

4.35   ■ QUESTIONING ● TO CHALLENGE ▼ CLIENT THOUGHT

4.37   ■ PARAPHRASING ● TO ACKNOWLEDGE ▼ CLIENT BEHAVIOR

4.39   ■ PLAYING A HUNCH ● TO CHALLENGE ▼ CLIENT EXPERIENCE

4.41   ■ GIVING FEEDBACK ● TO EXPLORE ▼ CLIENT BEHAVIOR plus IMMEDIACY

4.42   ■ QUESTIONING ● TO CHALLENGE ▼ CLIENT BEHAVIOR

4.44   ■ PARAPHRASING ● TO ACKNOWLEDGE ▼ CLIENT FEELING

4.46   ■ QUESTIONING ● TO CHALLENGE ▼ CLIENT BEHAVIOR

4.48   ■ QUESTIONING ● TO CHALLENGE ▼ CLIENT FEELING

4.50   ■ PARAPHRASING ● TO ACKNOWLEDGE ▼ CLIENT EXPERIENCE

4.52   ■ QUESTIONING ● TO CHALLENGE ▼ CLIENT EXPERIENCE

4.54   ■ QUESTIONING ● TO CHALLENGE ▼ CLIENT EXPERIENCE

4.56   ■ DIRECTING ● TO CHALLENGE ▼ CLIENT BEHAVIOR

4.58   ■ PARAPHRASING ● TO ACKNOWLEDGE ▼ CLIENT BEHAVIOR

4.60   ■ PARAPHRASING ● TO ACKNOWLEDGE ▼ CLIENT EXPERIENCE

4.62   ■ OPENING OR CLOSING ● TO ACKNOWLEDGE ▼ CLIENT EXPERIENCE

Exercise 5 for Videocassette:
Observe, Identify, Compare, and Reflect

Observe

View session 5 on the BCR videocassette.

Identify

Watch session 5 again, following the transcript below. Response, intent, and focus are not shown in the identification column. Stop the videocassette after each counselor response and fill in the identified response, intent, and focus.

This exercise calls for a total of 43 response (■), intent (●), and focus (▼) identifications.

Compare

Check suggested response, intent, and focus identifications for Exercise 5, following the reflection questions, to compare identified responses, intents, and focuses.

#	SPEAKER	VERBATIM RESPONSE/TRANSCRIPT	IDENTIFICATION
5.1	COUNSELOR:	"Okay, Theresa, where would you like to start today?"	■ _____ ● _____ ▼ _____
5.2	CLIENT:	(sigh) "I would like to start with looking at issues around dealing with confrontation and just conflict. I seem to just shy away from it or just run away from it, or ignore it."	

#	SPEAKER	VERBATIM RESPONSE/TRANSCRIPT	IDENTIFICATION
5.3	COUNSELOR:	"Okay, you shy away or ignore conflict."	■ _____ ● _____ ▼ _____
5.4	CLIENT:	"Yes, I do."	
5.5	COUNSELOR:	"Could you tell me more about that?"	■ _____ ● _____ ▼ _____
5.6	CLIENT:	"It brings up all kinds of feelings and emotions that I'm not able to sort out and address, so I don't say anything. Let's take for an example an . . . an emotional conflict."	
5.7	COUNSELOR:	(nods) "Uhmm."	■ _____ ● _____ ▼ _____
5.8	CLIENT:	"I don't—I just don't speak up, I'll sit there and cry before I'll . . . get out the anger or what I'm feeling or want to express anything. Then a lot of times I've avoided a lot of issues that I needed to have addressed because I didn't confront it."	
5.9	COUNSELOR:	"Okay, there are all of these emotions going on inside of you, and instead of speaking up you hold them inside, and you also avoid conflicts because of that."	■ _____ ● _____ ▼ _____
5.10	CLIENT:	"Yes."	
5.11	COUNSELOR:	"Okay, as you've talked to me about this, I'm wondering if you could talk about some specific instances of conflict?"	■ _____ ● _____ ▼ _____
5.12	CLIENT:	"I can only. . . to the point of the sixties . . . and . . . and the injustices around treatment of people."	
5.13	COUNSELOR:	"As you say this I can hear the emotion in your voice, I can see it in your face, your eyes tear up a little."	■ _____ ● _____ ▼ _____

#	SPEAKER	VERBATIM RESPONSE/TRANSCRIPT	IDENTIFICATION
5.14	CLIENT:	"I can . . . feel the emotions and pain."	
5.15	COUNSELOR:	"There is just so much inside of you right now as you talk to me."	■ _____ ● _____ ▼ _____
5.16	CLIENT:	"Yes."	
5.17	COUNSELOR:	"I'm wondering if you could just sit with that for a few minutes and just feel those emotions—and just feel them for a little while and allow them to be there?"	■ _____ ● _____ ▼ _____
5.18	CLIENT:	"Overwhelming . . . I guess when you see . . . when you see your own father . . . treated . . . as a boy . . . and he's my father, and I see him as a man, and when and I think when going . . . and it touching you even further with you know, your own child, the first child."	
5.19	COUNSELOR:	(nods)	■ _____ ● _____ ▼ _____
5.20	CLIENT:	"In a segregated hospital in the South and nurses walking in not even looking at you, they just know you're there and . . . when it's time for the baby to be born, the orderlies just came in and just flipped me right onto the gurney and no feeling, just like I was just a piece, another piece of meat. I was getting ready to have my baby . . . they act like they didn't want to touch me. . . . I left after birth, the baby was placed in a second-hand incubator 'cause she was premature."	
5.21	COUNSELOR:	(nods)	■ _____ ● _____ ▼ _____
5.22	CLIENT:	"And the heat regulator didn't work . . . and she was burned. I don't know . . . there was nothing you could say. You, . . . you just know that she was just another statistic."	

#	SPEAKER	VERBATIM RESPONSE/TRANSCRIPT	IDENTIFICATION
5.23	COUNSELOR:	"You know, I see the terrible sadness on your face and hear it in your eyes . . .	■ _____ ● _____ ▼ _____
5.24	COUNSELOR:	and I also get a sense of rage here."	■ _____ ● _____ ▼ _____
5.25	CLIENT:	"Oh my . . . I felt I had gotten to a point of where it didn't hurt so much. Uh, but it still hurts, I, I didn't realize it, how much it did hurt."	
5.26	COUNSELOR:	(nods)	■ _____ ● _____ ▼ _____
5.27	CLIENT:	"And when you see years of racial injustice . . . you know, what can you say?"	
5.28	COUNSELOR:	"The thing that I hear in a way most strongly—a couple of things—is one being treated like a side of beef."	■ _____ ● _____ ▼ _____
5.29	CLIENT:	"Yes."	
5.30	COUNSELOR:	"Having your baby burned . . ."	■ _____ ● _____ ▼ _____
5.31	CLIENT:	"Yes."	
5.32	COUNSELOR:	"And having all of these emotions inside you that are just so strong . . ."	■ _____ ● _____ ▼ _____
5.33	CLIENT:	"Yes."	
5.34	COUNSELOR:	"And not being able to do anything about it, needing to be silent, I guess	■ _____ ● _____ ▼ _____
5.35	COUNSELOR:	That's a real powerful image for me to hear. (extended pause)	■ _____ ● _____ ▼ _____
5.36	COUNSELOR:	What's going on for you right now?"	■ _____ ● _____ ▼ _____

#	SPEAKER	VERBATIM RESPONSE/TRANSCRIPT	IDENTIFICATION
5.37	CLIENT:	"Years of not being able to speak."	
5.38	COUNSELOR:	"Tell me about those years."	■ _____ ● _____ ▼ _____
5.39	CLIENT:	"You want to forget and move on. It's hard to talk about, though."	
5.40	COUNSELOR:	"Now I see some odd, different things happening. You say that and you smile."	■ _____ ● _____ ▼ _____
5.41	CLIENT:	"Yeah, 'cause I think I . . . I guess it's a way of avoiding pain, and you sit here and try to be clinical about what happened."	
5.42	COUNSELOR:	"Even being with you right now, I get a sense of you holding things in."	■ _____ ● _____ ▼ _____
5.43	CLIENT:	"I am, and I'm putting on the smile to hide."	
5.44	COUNSELOR:	"Let me ask you to do something different then, okay? If it's okay and safe, all right, I'm wondering if you could say, what you would like to say about those years."	■ _____ ● _____ ▼ _____
5.45	CLIENT:	(shakes head)	
5.46	COUNSELOR:	"I see you shake your head.	■ _____ ● _____ ▼ _____
5.47	COUNSELOR:	This is, this is too difficult for you, is it?"	■ _____ ● _____ ▼ _____
5.48	CLIENT:	"It's really stuck. It's just like it's caught in here (gestures toward chest), and it's caught in here and it won't come up."	
5.49	COUNSELOR:	"Yeah, I get a sense of just being with you that there's just so much caught inside of you that it feels to me like if you let it up, when would it stop, there's just so much.	■ _____ ● _____ ▼ _____

#	SPEAKER	VERBATIM RESPONSE/TRANSCRIPT	IDENTIFICATION
5.50	COUNSELOR:	Is that on target?"	■ _____ ● _____ ▼ _____
5.51	CLIENT:	"It's a lot."	
5.52	COUNSELOR:	"What's it like to be that stuck?"	■ _____ ● _____ ▼ _____
5.53	CLIENT:	"Well, after a while you . . . resign yourself that it's history. And that part of your life is over, and there's more to look forward to than looking back."	
5.54	COUNSELOR:	(nods)	■ _____ ● _____ ▼ _____
5.55	CLIENT:	"You want so much to believe that things are better."	
5.56	COUNSELOR:	"So on one hand, you know, you look at this as history and it's over, and on the other hand you have this almost terrible pain inside you."	■ _____ ● _____ ▼ _____
5.57	CLIENT:	"There's nothing to explain . . . what happened."	
5.58	COUNSELOR:	"You know, when you say that, what I thought it was that . . . I just want, it seems to me, you know, you say there is nothing to explain what happened, okay, and on some level I say to myself I wonder if I could ever really understand what happened—being a white man from the North—I just wonder if I could ever understand what happened to you.	■ _____ ● _____ ▼ _____
5.59	COUNSELOR:	What's it like right now talking about this for you?"	■ _____ ● _____ ▼ _____
5.60	CLIENT:	"It lets me know that I've—I've still got some—some issues to deal with around it."	

#	SPEAKER	VERBATIM RESPONSE/TRANSCRIPT	IDENTIFICATION
5.61	COUNSELOR:	"And now let me ask you a different question. What's that like for you to share that with me—to tell me this story?"	■ _____ ● _____ ▼ _____
5.62	CLIENT:	(sigh) "I told you the story for you to—to help you understand the conflict and confrontation and why it's difficult for me."	
5.63	COUNSELOR:	(nods)	■ _____ ● _____ ▼ _____
5.64	CLIENT:	"And I felt that would give you an example."	
5.65	COUNSELOR:	"Yeah, I, I, I think I get some sense of how difficult it is for you to be in confrontation, and again I keep coming back to that sense of in my mind, of, of powerlessness—of feeling that you don't have the ability to make some choices, you know.	■ _____ ● _____ ▼ _____
5.66	COUNSELOR:	And at the same time I also am thinking now that there is a sense of maybe even protection—that, that in responding in some of those ways it was how you got through difficult situations."	■ _____ ● _____ ▼ _____
5.67	CLIENT:	"Yes."	
5.68	COUNSELOR:	"And so now on some hand you've learned that behavior, and it doesn't work for you anymore."	■ _____ ● _____ ▼ _____
5.69	CLIENT:	"I know there's a lot of things that I'm going to have to confront as a single woman and . . . I don't know."	
5.70	COUNSELOR:	"Okay, we just have a few minutes left here, all right? And I'm wondering how you would like to, to summarize the session—what did it mean for you today to be with me?"	■ _____ ● _____ ▼ _____

#	SPEAKER	VERBATIM RESPONSE/TRANSCRIPT	IDENTIFICATION
5.71	CLIENT:	"It helped me to raise a theme in my life. An ongoing theme that I just need to kind of work on."	
5.72	COUNSELOR:	"Could you, could you name that theme?"	■ _____ ● _____ ▼ _____
5.73	CLIENT:	"The theme is—I see more than one theme, but I know it's, ah, avoid confrontation, avoid conflict, possibly low self-esteem, and . . . maybe just those three is enough for right now."	
5.74	COUNSELOR:	"Okay, and the, and the other thing that I hear, Theresa, is sort of a connection between the discrimination, and how you were treated as a young woman, and the conflicts that you kind of needed to avoid then, and how you avoid conflicts today and how painful it is for you to be in conflicts today."	■ _____ ● _____ ▼ _____
5.75	CLIENT:	(nods)	
5.76	COUNSELOR:	"And what would you like to say to finish right now, Theresa?"	■ _____ ● _____ ▼ _____
5.77	CLIENT:	"I can't say anything."	
5.78	COUNSELOR:	"Okay, thank you very much, and so I'll see you next week."	■ _____ ● _____ ▼ _____
5.79	CLIENT:	"Okay."	

Reflect

1. At 5.58, the counselor says:

    "You know, when you say that, what I thought it was that . . . I just want, it seems to me, you know, you say there is nothing to explain what happened, okay, and on some level I say to myself I wonder if I could ever really understand what happened—being a white man from the North—I just wonder if I could ever understand what happened to you."

    What is your reaction to how the counselor is responding to the ethnic and gender variables in the client/counselor relationship?

2. How does the counselor respond to the client's nonverbal behavior?

Suggested Response, Intent, and Focus Identifications for Exercise 5

5.1   ■ <u>OPENING OR CLOSING</u> ● <u>TO EXPLORE</u> ▼ <u>CLIENT EXPERIENCE</u>

5.3   ■ <u>PARAPHRASING</u> ● <u>TO ACKNOWLEDGE</u> ▼ <u>CLIENT BEHAVIOR</u>

5.5   ■ <u>CLARIFYING</u> ● <u>TO EXPLORE</u> ▼ <u>CLIENT BEHAVIOR</u>

5.7   ■ <u>ATTENDING</u> ● <u>TO ACKNOWLEDGE</u> ▼ <u>CLIENT EXPERIENCE</u>

5.9   ■ <u>PARAPHRASING</u> ● <u>TO ACKNOWLEDGE</u> ▼ <u>CLIENT FEELING</u>

5.11 ■ <u>CLARIFYING</u> ● <u>TO EXPLORE</u> ▼ <u>CLIENT EXPERIENCE</u>

5.13 ■ <u>GIVING FEEDBACK</u> ● <u>TO ACKNOWLEDGE</u> ▼ <u>CLIENT BEHAVIOR</u>

5.15 ■ <u>EMPATHIZING</u> ● <u>TO ACKNOWLEDGE</u> ▼ <u>CLIENT FEELING</u> plus <u>IMMEDIACY</u>

5.17 ■ <u>DIRECTING</u> ● <u>TO ACKNOWLEDGE</u> ▼ <u>CLIENT FEELING</u>

5.19 ■ <u>ATTENDING</u> ● <u>TO ACKNOWLEDGE</u> ▼ <u>CLIENT EXPERIENCE</u>

5.21 ■ <u>ATTENDING</u> ● <u>TO ACKNOWLEDGE</u> ▼ <u>CLIENT EXPERIENCE</u>

5.23   ■ <u>GIVING FEEDBACK</u> ● <u>TO ACKNOWLEDGE</u> ▼ <u>CLIENT BEHAVIOR</u>

5.24   ■ <u>PLAYING A HUNCH</u> ● <u>TO CHALLENGE</u> ▼ <u>CLIENT FEELING</u>

5.26   ■ <u>ALLOWING SILENCE</u> ● <u>TO ACKNOWLEDGE</u> ▼ <u>CLIENT FEELING</u>

5.28   ■ <u>PARAPHRASING</u> ● <u>TO ACKNOWLEDGE</u> ▼ <u>CLIENT EXPERIENCE</u>

5.30   ■ <u>PARAPHRASING</u> ● <u>TO ACKNOWLEDGE</u> ▼ <u>CLIENT EXPERIENCE</u>

5.32   ■ <u>EMPATHIZING</u> ● <u>TO ACKNOWLEDGE</u> ▼ <u>CLIENT FEELING</u>

5.34   ■ <u>PLAYING A HUNCH</u> ● <u>TO CHALLENGE</u> ▼ <u>CLIENT BEHAVIOR</u>

5.35   ■ <u>SELF-DISCLOSING</u> ● <u>TO ACKNOWLEDGE</u> ▼ <u>CLIENT BEHAVIOR</u>

5.36   ■ <u>QUESTIONING</u> ● <u>TO CHALLENGE</u> ▼ <u>CLIENT FEELING plus IMMEDIACY</u>

5.38   ■ <u>CLARIFYING</u> ● <u>TO EXPLORE</u> ▼ <u>CLIENT EXPERIENCE</u>

5.40   ■ <u>NOTING A DISCREPANCY</u> ● <u>TO CHALLENGE</u> ▼ <u>CLIENT BEHAVIOR</u>

5.42   ■ <u>PLAYING A HUNCH</u> ● <u>TO CHALLENGE</u> ▼ <u>CLIENT BEHAVIOR plus IMMEDIACY</u>

5.44   ■ <u>DIRECTING</u> ● <u>TO CHALLENGE</u> ▼ <u>CLIENT EXPERIENCE</u>

5.46   ■ <u>GIVING FEEDBACK</u> ● <u>TO ACKNOWLEDGE</u> ▼ <u>CLIENT BEHAVIOR</u>

5.47   ■ <u>QUESTIONING</u> ● <u>TO EXPLORE</u> ▼ <u>CLIENT FEELING</u>

5.49   ■ <u>PLAYING A HUNCH</u> ● <u>TO CHALLENGE</u> ▼ <u>CLIENT FEELING</u>

5.50   ■ <u>QUESTIONING</u> ● <u>TO EXPLORE</u> ▼ <u>CLIENT EXPERIENCE</u>

5.52   ■ <u>QUESTIONING</u> ● <u>TO EXPLORE</u> ▼ <u>CLIENT FEELING</u>

5.54   ■ <u>ALLOWING SILENCE</u> ● <u>TO ACKNOWLEDGE</u> ▼ <u>CLIENT EXPERIENCE</u>

5.56   ■ <u>NOTING A DISCREPANCY</u> ● <u>TO CHALLENGE</u> ▼ <u>CLIENT FEELING</u>

5.58   ■ <u>SELF-DISCLOSING</u> ● <u>TO ACKNOWLEDGE</u> ▼ <u>CLIENT EXPERIENCE</u>

5.59   ■ <u>QUESTIONING</u> ● <u>TO EXPLORE</u> ▼ <u>CLIENT EXPERIENCE plus IMMEDIACY</u>

5.61   ■ <u>QUESTIONING</u> ● <u>TO EXPLORE</u> ▼ <u>CLIENT EXPERIENCE plus IMMEDIACY</u>

5.63   ■ <u>ATTENDING</u> ● <u>TO ACKNOWLEDGE</u> ▼ <u>CLIENT EXPERIENCE</u>

5.65   ■ <u>NOTING A THEME</u> ● <u>TO CHALLENGE</u> ▼ <u>CLIENT EXPERIENCE</u>

5.66   ■ <u>REFRAMING</u> ● <u>TO CHALLENGE</u> ▼ <u>CLIENT EXPERIENCE</u>

5.68   ■ <u>PLAYING A HUNCH</u> ● <u>TO CHALLENGE</u> ▼ <u>CLIENT THOUGHT</u>

5.70   ■ <u>QUESTIONING</u> ● <u>TO ACKNOWLEDGE</u> ▼ <u>CLIENT EXPERIENCE plus IMMEDIACY</u>

5.72   ■ <u>QUESTIONING</u> ● <u>TO CHALLENGE</u> ▼ <u>CLIENT THOUGHT</u>

5.74   ■ <u>NOTING A CONNECTION</u> ● <u>TO CHALLENGE</u> ▼ <u>CLIENT EXPERIENCE</u>

5.76   ■ <u>QUESTIONING</u> ● <u>TO EXPLORE</u> ▼ <u>CLIENT EXPERIENCE plus IMMEDIACY</u>

5.78   ■ <u>OPENING OR CLOSING</u> ● <u>TO ACKNOWLEDGE</u> ▼ <u>CLIENT EXPERIENCE</u>

Exercise 6 for Videocassette: Observe, Create, Compare, and Reflect

Observe

Watch session 6, following the transcript below. Stop the videocassette after the response from the client in the three selected (shaded) client/counselor interactions.

Create

For each selected client/counselor interaction, fill in a student-created verbatim response that exemplifies the given response, intent, and focus identification.

This exercise calls for three student-created counselor responses. Each student-created response should be in reaction to what the client has just said. However, the client response may not follow the student-created response.

Compare

The actual counselor responses for the selected examples are provided in Actual Counselor Responses for Exercise 6, following the reflection questions. Discuss the student-created responses in supervision and with other students.

#	SPEAKER	VERBATIM RESPONSES/TRANSCRIPT	IDENTIFICATION
6.1	COUNSELOR:	"Sonja, how would you like to spend our time today?"	■ OPENING OR CLOSING ● TO ACKNOWLEDGE ▼ CLIENT EXPERIENCE

#	SPEAKER	VERBATIM RESPONSE/TRANSCRIPT	IDENTIFICATION
6.2	CLIENT:	"Well, I'm struggling with an issue with my sister. I feel like it's something I've been working on a long time and I keep making progress, but I want to make more progress with it. I'm sort of at a point where I'm ready to move forward . . . and I don't know how to do that. I'm feeling ready to go, but I don't know how to get there."	
6.3	COUNSELOR:	"You said you were struggling with an issue and you don't know how to move forward."	■ PARAPHRASING ● TO ACKNOWLEDGE ▼ CLIENT BEHAVIOR
6.4	COUNSELOR:	"So how is it for you to have this type of feeling?"	■ QUESTIONING ● TO EXPLORE ▼ CLIENT FEELING
6.5	CLIENT:	"Frustrating. It feels sort of like this tug-of-war, because I know that it's possible, but I'm feeling kind of stuck. And it's complicated for me because she's my twin sister and I think it's always harder to deal with issues with a twin—a fraternal twin, so we're not identical, not alike in personality and things like that, but . . ."	
6.6	COUNSELOR:	"You mentioned that you felt stuck and you were struggling a little bit.	■ PARAPHRASING ● TO ACKNOWLEDGE ▼ CLIENT BEHAVIOR
6.7	COUNSELOR:	Can you tell me a little bit more about being stuck?"	■ QUESTIONING ● TO EXPLORE ▼ CLIENT EXPERIENCE
6.8	CLIENT:	"Um, it's hard for me to . . . I think I feel stuck because it's hard for me to imagine very clearly what something different would be like in my relationship with her. So I can't get ahold of this new place to go to."	
6.9	COUNSELOR:	Create a counselor response.	■ CLARIFYING ● TO EXPLORE ▼ CLIENT EXPERIENCE

#	SPEAKER	VERBATIM RESPONSE/TRANSCRIPT	IDENTIFICATION
6.10	CLIENT:	"Um, well, in my relationship with her. . . she has emotional and physical needs and she's struggling with a lot of those right now, she's making . . . there are a lot of demands put upon me by her and yet, a lot of them feel pretty manipulative and that kind of thing. It's hard for me to sort out what are her real needs and what I need to step back from, take care of myself by not getting kind of absorbed into or swallowed into. So I guess that's the stuckness. I don't know, it's hard to sort that out and I end up feeling kind of guilty or disloyal. And she's kind of good at playing on that."	
6.11	COUNSELOR:	"Sonja, I know we spoke briefly about your sister and some underlying conflicts that were going on.	■ PARAPHRASING ● TO ACKNOWLEDGE ▼ CLIENT EXPERIENCE
6.12	COUNSELOR:	But could it be something else going on with that?"	■ QUESTIONING ● TO CHALLENGE ▼ CLIENT EXPERIENCE
6.13	CLIENT:	"Well, you know when I have really sat and sat with it and thought more about it, I've really realized that there's a kind of fearful feeling or sort of scared. I think I know that because that's the feeling I get. I mean I have this gut-wrenching thing that goes on and I know what that is for me. It's some kind of fear. I think it's both that she might go away. But I don't think she would, but somehow think if I am not really nice to her that could happen. But I also think there's a sort of a fear about not taking care of myself too in this and uh . . ."	
6.14	COUNSELOR:	Create a counselor response.	■ PARAPHRASING ● TO ACKNOWLEDGE ▼ CLIENT EXPERIENCE

#	SPEAKER	VERBATIM RESPONSE/TRANSCRIPT	IDENTIFICATION
6.15	CLIENT:	"That I'll be disappointed in myself in not taking better care of myself in this situation in a way that feels good to me. Not finding a way to kind of be in a relationship with her, but take care of myself in the relationship better. I think I'm kind of afraid of both things. But at the same time when I start to imagine being more direct with her, I let her know my limits, but I don't do it as directly and clearly as I think I could and things like that. When I think about that and doing that, I think 'Well, I could really do that.' I mean there isn't anything awful about that. Nothing, nothing awful is going to happen. It will probably be fine, but it's hard to get, it's hard to move to that place."	
6.16	COUNSELOR:	"I hear you saying on one hand that you're afraid to cause a conflict with your sister because you fear that she would leave. On the other hand, you're saying that you want to help yourself and to get to the bottom of the conflict, but there is an amount of fear there."	■ NOTING A DISCREPANCY ● TO CHALLENGE ▼ CLIENT FEELING
6.17	COUNSELOR:	"So, could you tell me what you've done to bring these two pieces together?"	■ QUESTIONING ● TO CHALLENGE ▼ CLIENT BEHAVIOR
6.18	CLIENT:	"Well, the first thing I'm doing with it is to see it. That helps me a lot, because once I see it then I can say to myself, 'Now you know what it is.' If I don't know what it is and it's kind of rumbling around back there, some gut feeling that I can't get a sense of it, I feel kind of lost. So, I don't feel as lost now that I have a sense of some fear there and what that's kind of connected to. Because I can look at it more realistically and I go, 'Well she's not really going to go away. She's going to be unhappy, but she's already unhappy	

#	SPEAKER	VERBATIM RESPONSE/TRANSCRIPT	IDENTIFICATION
		with the way things go.' So then the issue for me is to be okay with letting her, not letting her, but that I'm okay with that—how she responds. If I feel that I've done, if I've done things that have integrity for me. That I'm still present for her, but I'm not there to be stepped on and walked on, talked to in certain ways, things like that."	
6.19	COUNSELOR:	Create a counselor response.	■ OPENING OR CLOSING ● TO ACKNOWLEDGE ▼ CLIENT EXPERIENCE
6.20	CLIENT:	"Yes, I would."	

Reflect

1. What might the client say in reaction to the student-created response at 6.9?

2. What might the client say in reaction to the student-created response at 6.14?

3. What might the client say in reaction to the student-created response at 6.19?

Actual Counselor Responses for Exercise 6

6.9   "This new place . . ."

6.14   "Fear of not taking care of yourself—could you tell me?"

6.19   "This ends our session for this week. Would you like to continue with this next week?"

Exercise 7 for Videocassette:
Observe, Identify, Create, Compare, and Reflect

Observe

Watch session 7, following the transcript below. Stop the videocassette after the response from the client in the five selected (shaded) client/counselor interactions.

Identify and Create

For the selected client/counselor interactions, identify an appropriate counseling response, intent, and focus in the identification column (for example, questioning/to explore/ client thought plus immediacy). Then, fill in a student-created counselor response that exemplifies the identified response, intent, and focus ("What are you thinking about right now as we talk?").

This exercise calls for five response (■), intent (●), and focus (▼) identifications and five corresponding student-created counselor responses. Each student-created verbatim response should be in reaction to what the client has just said. However, the client response may not follow the student-created verbatim response.

Compare

The actual counselor responses for the selected examples and a suggested identification of the response, intent, and focus for each actual counselor response are provided in Actual Counselor Responses and Suggested Response, Intent, and Focus Identifications for Exercise 7, following the reflection questions. Discuss the student-created identifications and counseling responses in supervision and with other students.

#	SPEAKER	VERBATIM RESPONSE/TRANSCRIPT	IDENTIFICATION
7.1	CLIENT:	"Well, . . . still concerned about the situation with my mom. Haven't talked to the family yet, but I am, I really, to me, there's a sense of urgency about this because every day that she's driving there's a possibility of something happening. And that's really scary for me, to have to kind of carry that around."	
7.2	COUNSELOR:	"And you carry around this scariness about your mom driving because . . ."	■ QUESTIONING ● TO CHALLENGE ▼ CLIENT FEELING
7.3	CLIENT:	"Because I feel responsible for her safety and the people she comes in contact with."	
7.4	COUNSELOR:	Create a counselor response.	Identify counseling response, intent, and focus ■ _____ ● _____ ▼ _____
7.5	CLIENT:	"Because I'm the only one that seems to be concerned about it. Other people are kind of caught up in what goes on in their daily lives and not really, I don't think, taking the time to evaluate it properly. So . . ."	
7.6	COUNSELOR:	"In the last session I heard you use the word 'caretaker,' and now I hear—again I hear you say you're the only one that's really, truly concerned.	■ GIVING FEEDBACK ● TO CHALLENGE ▼ CLIENT BEHAVIOR
7.7	COUNSELOR:	I'm wondering how that is for you to be the only one in the family that seems concerned about this?"	■ QUESTIONING ● TO CHALLENGE ▼ CLIENT FEELING
7.8	CLIENT:	"It's frustrating, it just—it feels like a big responsibility for me to be the one that's responsible for her safety, knowing that you know that she's okay."	

#	SPEAKER	VERBATIM RESPONSE/TRANSCRIPT	IDENTIFICATION
7.9	COUNSELOR:	Create a counselor response.	Identify a counseling response, intent, and focus. ■ _____ ● _____ ▼ _____
7.10	CLIENT:	"Well, I think that my mother would probably go on driving until something happened. And if we sat down all together and determined that maybe she's not safe driving anymore that we could present to her that as a family, or maybe have her included in a decision-making process that maybe driving is a little too hazardous for her and that we should look at some options."	
7.11	COUNSELOR:	"I'm hearing the rest of the family—and I am being confrontive here—but I'm hearing the rest of the family say things are fine, and Mom says things are fine, and the only person I'm hearing real concerned about this is you. I'm kind of puzzled about that."	■ NOTING A DISCREPANCY ● TO CHALLENGE ▼ CLIENT FEELING
7.12	CLIENT:	"My concern is that the others aren't taking time to think about it and they're not really seeing the risks here. And the same thing with my mom, that her independence is so important that she is not willing to pay the price of having some of the independence taken away in order for her to be safe and those around her to be safe."	
7.13	COUNSELOR:	Create a counselor response.	Identify a counseling response, intent, and focus. ■ _____ ● _____ ▼ _____

#	SPEAKER	VERBATIM RESPONSE/TRANSCRIPT	IDENTIFICATION
7.14	CLIENT:	"I . . . yeah, I would feel a lot safer, sure, if I knew that she wasn't going to be hurt or that other people weren't going to be hurt. It would be a tremendous burden lifted off of me."	
7.15	COUNSELOR:	"How is it for you when I put this back on you and kind of confront it. Maybe it's not them or her, maybe it has to do with you."	■ QUESTIONING ● TO CHALLENGE ▼ CLIENT FEELING plus IMMEDIACY
7.16	CLIENT:	"I'm realizing that if she were to not drive how much freer it would be for me that I wouldn't have to worry that was she was okay, and that I would feel safer."	
7.17	COUNSELOR:	Create a counselor response.	Identify a counseling response, intent, and focus. ■ _____ ● _____ ▼ _____
7.18	CLIENT:	"Yeah, my sisters are a lot older than I am and I am the baby of the family and so Mom and I have this really special relationship, so it would be a big loss for me if I were to lose her. And I, I think . . ."	
7.19	COUNSELOR:	Create a counselor response.	Identify a counseling response, intent, and focus. ■ _____ ● _____ ▼ _____
7.20	CLIENT:	"Mmm . . . yeah, that's a fear of mine."	
7.21	COUNSELOR:	"What's going on right now?"	■ QUESTIONING ● TO CHALLENGE ▼ CLIENT FEELING plus IMMEDIACY

#	SPEAKER	VERBATIM RESPONSE/TRANSCRIPT	IDENTIFICATION
7.22	CLIENT:	"It's hard. She was the oldest of five and everyone else in her family is gone. My uncle died about two years ago, and so I've been concerned about her leaving as well, her passing away as well and that's, that would be a big loss for me."	
7.23	COUNSELOR:	"I can see your eyes tear up, and your energy kind of shifts."	■ GIVING FEEDBACK ● TO ACKNOWLEDGE ▼ CLIENT BEHAVIOR
7.24	CLIENT:	"Yeah, it's hard. It's easier to concentrate on the safety issue with my mother than to really look at the possibility of losing her. That is probably closer to the real issue."	

Reflect

How do the student-created counselor responses in this exercise exemplify the definition of counseling (from Part 1, p. 5)?

Counseling is an interaction in which the counselor focuses on client experience, client feeling, client thought, and client behavior with intentional responses to acknowledge, to explore, or to challenge.

Counseling has specific goals, the *first* of which is to facilitate awareness. This is achieved by keeping the focus on the client, acknowledging feelings, experience, and behavior. By exploring feelings and behavior and future options, the *second* counseling goal, healthy decision making, can be maximized. Further exploration and challenging can lead to the *third* goal of counseling, appropriate action, resulting in more fulfilling personal and social functioning.

1. Student-created response at 7.4:

2. Student-created response at 7.9:

3. Student-created response at 7.13:

4. Student-created response at 7.17:

5. Student-created response at 7.19:

Actual Counselor Responses and Suggested Response,
Intent, and Focus Identifications for Exercise 7

COUNSELOR:

7.4   "And you are responsible for her safety because . . ."

■ QUESTIONING ● TO CHALLENGE ▼ CLIENT FEELING

7.9   "I'm just kind of confused about why you're—how it is that you're responsible for that? Can you help me understand that a little better?"

■ QUESTIONING ● TO CHALLENGE ▼ CLIENT FEELING

7.13   "If Mom stops driving, it feels like it, she may not get what she wants, but I'm hearing that it might make you feel safer. I'm wondering if there's any accuracy in that?"

■ PLAYING A HUNCH ● TO CHALLENGE ▼ CLIENT FEELING

7.17   "So when I kind of give this back to you, it helps you be aware that some of this is about you and not so much about her."

■ PARAPHRASING ● TO ACKNOWLEDGE ▼ CLIENT EXPERIENCE

7.19   "Let me stop you there for a minute. I am wondering how much this is about Mom not driving and how much this is about your mom's 85 and losing Mom."

■ PLAYING A HUNCH ● TO CHALLENGE ▼ CLIENT EXPERIENCE

EXERCISES 8–15 FOR STUDENT SELF-TAPING

Exercise 8:
Practice, Observe, Identify, and Reflect

Practice

Videotape a 15-minute session with a partner who takes on the role of client; practice using the counseling responses.

Observe

View the video.

Identify

Use the Counselor Response Identification Form (CRIF) in Appendix A to identify as many counseling responses, intents, and focuses as possible.

Reflect

Describe the experience of viewing yourself as counselor in the videotaped session.

Exercise 9:
Practice, Observe, Identify, and Reflect

Practice

Videotape a 15-minute session with a partner who takes on the role of client; practice using the counseling responses.

Observe

View the video.

Identify

Use the CRIF in Appendix A to identify as many counseling responses, intents, and focuses as possible.

Reflect

Compare the experience of being a counselor in this session with the previous session.

Exercise 10:
Demonstrate, Observe, Identify, and Reflect

Demonstrate

With a partner who takes on the role of client, videotape a 20-minute session in which you demonstrate the following:

1. The *essential* responses
        Opening or closing
        Attending
2. Any of the *passive* responses
        Empathizing
        Paraphrasing
        Giving feedback
3. A discretionary response
        Allowing silence

Observe

View the video.

Identify

Use the CRIF in Appendix A to identify as many counseling responses, intents, and focuses as possible.

Reflect

Discuss age, gender, ethnic, and other relevant client and counselor variables and how they may influence the client/counselor relationship.

Exercise 11:
Demonstrate, Observe, Identify, and Reflect

Demonstrate

With a partner who takes on the role of client, videotape a 20-minute session in which you demonstrate the following:

1. The *essential* responses
   Opening or closing
   Attending
2. Any of the *active* responses
   Clarifying
   Directing
   Questioning
3. Any of the *passive* responses
   Empathizing
   Paraphrasing
   Giving feedback

Observe

View the video.

Identify

Use the CRIF in Appendix A to identify as many counseling responses, intents, and focuses as possible.

Reflect

If you could do this session again, what would you do differently?

Exercise 12:
Demonstrate, Observe, Identify, and Reflect

Demonstrate

With a partner who takes on the role of client, videotape a 20-minute session in which you demonstrate the following:

1. The *essential* responses
    Opening and closing
    Attending
2. Any of the *interpretive* responses
    Playing a hunch
    Noting a theme
    Noting a discrepancy
    Noting a connection
    Reframing
3. Any of the *active* responses
    Clarifying
    Directing
    Questioning
4. Any of the *passive* responses
    Empathizing
    Paraphrasing
    Giving feedback
5. A *discretionary* response
    Self-disclosing

Observe

View the video.

Identify

Use the CRIF in Appendix A to identify as many counseling responses, intents, and focuses as possible.

Reflect

Discuss what you feel you were doing well in this session.

Exercise 13:
Demonstrate, Observe, Identify, and Reflect

Demonstrate

With a partner who takes on the role of client, videotape a 30-minute session in which you demonstrate the following intent and focus, using appropriate counseling responses.

1. Intent: to acknowledge
2. Focus: client experience

Observe

View the video.

Identify

Use the CRIF in Appendix A to identify as many counseling responses, intents, and focuses as possible.

Reflect

Discuss how you see yourself being reflective, respectful, concrete, and genuine.

Exercise 14: Demonstrate, Observe, Identify, and Reflect

Demonstrate

With a partner who takes on the role of client, videotape a 30-minute session in which you demonstrate the following intents and focuses, using appropriate counseling responses.

1. Intent
    To acknowledge
    To explore
2. Focus
    Client experience
    Client feeling, client thought, or client behavior

Observe

View the video.

Identify

Use the CRIF in Appendix A to identify as many counseling responses, intents, and focuses as possible.

Reflect

Name specific counseling responses, intents, and focuses that seem to work best for you as a counselor. Speculate on why this is so.

Exercise 15:
Demonstrate, Observe, Identify, and Reflect

Demonstrate

With a partner who takes on the role of client, videotape a 30-minute session in which you demonstrate the following intents and focuses, using appropriate counseling responses.

1. Intent
    To acknowledge
    To explore
    To challenge
2. Focus
    Client experience
    Client feeling, client thought, or client behavior plus immediacy

Observe

View the video.

Identify

Use the CRIF in Appendix A to identify as many counseling responses, intents, and focuses as possible.

Reflect

Reflect on what you have learned from the 15 exercises.

APPENDIX A

TABLE 1
RESPONSES AND ASSOCIATED INTENTS AND FOCUSES

RESPONSE ■	INTENT ●	FOCUS ▼
ESSENTIAL: Opening or closing Attending	Opening almost always to explore; sometimes to acknowledge. Closing almost always to acknowledge. Both could be to challenge.	Almost always client experience, because these are generally nonspecific responses. Immediacy may be an additional focus.
PASSIVE: Empathizing Paraphrasing Giving feedback	Almost always to acknowledge; sometimes to explore or to challenge.	Specific to the response. Immediacy often used.
ACTIVE: Clarifying Directing Questioning	Never to acknowledge; almost always to explore; sometimes to challenge.	Varies. Immediacy often used.
INTERPRETIVE: Playing a hunch Noting a theme Noting a discrepancy Noting a connection Reframing	Almost always to challenge.	Generally more specific: client thought, client feeling, or client behavior. May be multiple, especially for noting a discrepancy. Immediacy often used.
DISCRETIONARY: Allowing silence Self-disclosing	Not always apparent. Allowing silence may be to explore, but could be to challenge. Self-disclosing may be to acknowledge, to explore, or to challenge.	Not always apparent, because allowing silence is nonspecific. Self-disclosing may seem to not focus on client, but should be related to client thought, client feeling, or client behavior. Immediacy often used in a follow-up response to self-disclosing.

TABLE 2
QUICK REFERENCE: RESPONSES, INTENTS, FOCUSES

<table>
<tr><th></th><th></th><th>DESCRIPTION</th><th>EXAMPLE</th></tr>
<tr><td rowspan="13">RESPONSE</td><td>OPENING OR CLOSING</td><td>Beginning or ending a session</td><td>"Where would you like to start today?"</td></tr>
<tr><td>ATTENDING</td><td>Eye contact, open posture</td><td></td></tr>
<tr><td>EMPATHIZING</td><td>Stating what the client is feeling</td><td>"You feel angry right now."</td></tr>
<tr><td>PARAPHRASING</td><td>Stating the essence of what the client is saying</td><td>"You have come to counseling to talk about your math anxiety."</td></tr>
<tr><td>GIVING FEEDBACK</td><td>Stating what has been observed</td><td>"You frowned when you said that."</td></tr>
<tr><td>CLARIFYING</td><td>Asking the client to be more concrete</td><td>"Tell me more about that."</td></tr>
<tr><td>DIRECTING</td><td>Changing the direction of the session or giving a directive</td><td>"Stay with that thought."</td></tr>
<tr><td>QUESTIONING</td><td>Asking a question</td><td>"What could you do to make this better for you?"</td></tr>
<tr><td>PLAYING A HUNCH</td><td>Presenting a possible interpretation</td><td>"I have a sense that this is more important to you than you are saying."</td></tr>
<tr><td>NOTING A THEME</td><td>Presenting an ongoing theme or pattern</td><td>"Your sense of dissatisfaction is a theme in everything you talk about."</td></tr>
<tr><td>NOTING A DISCREPANCY</td><td>Presenting two things that do not seem to fit</td><td>"There seems to be a discrepancy between the sadness you feel and the smile on your face."</td></tr>
<tr><td>NOTING A CONNECTION</td><td>Presenting two things that do seem to fit</td><td>"There seems to be a connection between the people you are associating with and the conflict you are feeling."</td></tr>
</table>

		DESCRIPTION	EXAMPLE
RESPONSE	REFRAMING	Stating an alternative way of viewing	"Another way of looking at this is that you have learned a valuable lesson."
	ALLOWING SILENCE	Giving the client time to process and continue	
	SELF-DISCLOSING	Sharing personal information	"When that happened to me, I felt betrayed."
INTENT	TO ACKNOWLEDGE	Wanting the client to know that the client has been heard	See Paraphrasing.
	TO EXPLORE	Wanting the client to expand on what the client has been talking about	See Questioning.
	TO CHALLENGE	Wanting the client to view his/her situation differently	See Noting a discrepancy.
FOCUS	CLIENT EXPERIENCE	Broadest focus	See Clarifying.
	CLIENT FEELING	Emotion	See Empathizing.
	CLIENT THOUGHT	Cognition	See Directing.
	CLIENT BEHAVIOR	What the client is doing	See Giving feedback.
	IMMEDIACY	Here and now added to another focus	See Empathizing.

TABLE 3
COMPARING BASIC COUNSELING RESPONSES TO RESPONSES/SKILLS OF OTHER MODELS

	MODELS				
	BCR	KOTTLER	EGAN	IVEY	OKUN
RESPONSE	Opening or closing				
	Attending	Active listening	Attending and listening	Attending/ Observation skills	Responsive listening
	Empathizing	Empathy	Basic empathy	Reflection of feeling Content/Meaning	Reflecting
	Paraphrasing			Summarizing	Paraphrasing
	Giving feedback	Confrontation	Feedback	Feedback Influencing	Confrontation
	Clarifying		Clarification/ Prompting	Encouraging	Clarifying Probing
	Directing			Directives	
	Questioning	Questioning	Probing	Prompting/ Probing/ Encouraging Open/Closed questions	Probing
	Noting a connection		Connections		
	Noting a theme		Themes		
	Noting a discrepancy		Interpretation	Confrontation Interpretation	
	Reframing			Interpretations	
	Playing a hunch	Confrontation	Advanced empathy		Confrontation Checking out
	Allowing silence				(Minimal verbal responses)
	Self-disclosing	Confrontation Self-disclosure		Self-disclosure	Confrontation
INTENT	To acknowledge				
	To explore		Explore		
	To challenge		Challenge		
FOCUS	Client experience		Focusing	Focusing	
	Client feeling		Focusing	Focusing	Checking out
	Client thought		Focusing	Focusing	
	Client behavior		Focusing	Focusing	
	Immediacy	Immediacy			Checking out
OTHER				Advice/ Information	Informing
				Giving instructions	
				Logical consequences	
			Screening		
		Reinforcing	Support		
		Goal setting			
		Modeling			

COUNSELOR RESPONSE IDENTIFICATION FORM (CRIF) FOR EXERCISES 8–15

STUDENT/COUNSELOR: EXERCISE #:

SESSION #   DATE:

1. *VERBATIM* of counselor/client interaction. Include what was said by the client before and after what was said by the counselor. Add additional verbatim if necessary.

    CLIENT:

    COUNSELOR:

    CLIENT:

2. *IDENTIFY*

    ■ RESPONSE:

    ● INTENT:

    ▼ FOCUS:

3. *ALTERNATIVE COUNSELOR RESPONSE*

4. *IDENTIFY THE ALTERNATIVE COUNSELOR RESPONSE*

    ■ RESPONSE:

    ● INTENT:

    ▼ FOCUS:

5. *QUESTIONS OR COMMENTS*

APPENDIX B

CD-ROM Help

Selecting a Session

To begin working with the *Basic Counseling Responses* CD-ROM, you must select a session.

Click on a session number (1 through 7) to select a counseling session. Once a session is selected, a still image from the session will display in the video window. To choose a different session, simply click another session number. (However, if you have selected a session and have worked on its associated exercise or reflection questions, you will not be able to select a new session until you save or do not save the work for the selected session.)

You may observe (watch the counseling session with the response, intent, and focus identification shown or hidden), you may do the exercise for the session, or you may reflect on the session by answering a few questions. To choose one of these three options, click either the Observe tab, the Exercise tab, or the Reflect tab shown at the top of the screen. If you are not sure which option to choose, you may want to watch the Introduction again by clicking Repeat Intro.

After you select a session, you may click Get Saved Work to continue previous work on the exercise or reflection questions for this session (this assumes you worked on this session previously and saved your work to the computer's hard drive or a floppy disk). After you click Get Saved Work, you will be prompted for the disk and directory location of your previously saved work. In your list of files, you may see text files ending in ".TXT" and saved files ending in ".BCR". Select a saved file from the list to reload the work it contains (".TXT" files are to be printed and ".BCR" files are to be reloaded).

If problems are encountered during reload, you will be informed in the message area in the lower portion of the screen. Normally, you will see the message "Saved work successfully loaded." You may then continue working where you left off when you saved the work to a floppy disk.

A typical interaction might be:

1. Click the Session tab.
2. Click a Session sidebar (numbered 1-7) to select a session.

(Observe, Exercise, and Reflect tabs become available.)

Observing a Session

You may observe all or part of the session you selected. By default, the response, intent, and focus identification will be hidden. If you want to show the identified response, intent, and focus, click Show. They will be shown in the spaces below the video window when the counselor is responding. If you want to hide the response, intent, and focus, click Hide.

To change the volume of the session, click the Volume button in the lower right corner of the screen. Click the Up Arrow to increase the volume and the Down Arrow to lower it. When you reach maximum or minimum volume, the arrow will turn gray. If an acceptable volume cannot be found, you may need to exit the CD-ROM and change the system volume of your computer. You may then restart the CD-ROM and you will likely have a more acceptable range of volume control.

A video controller bar is located directly below the observe video window. This controller can be used to control the video while observing. You will find many of the controls are similar to those found on a VCR. From left to right, the bar contains the following controls:

Volume—do not use. Video sound can best be controlled using the volume control in the lower right corner of the observe screen.

Play/Stop—click the right-facing triangle to play the session and the double vertical bar to stop the session. This control "toggles" between play and stop as you click it. Use this control to pause the session if you wish.

Progress Bar—click anywhere along the wide bar to reposition the video at a desired point in the session. The full length of the slider represents the full length of the session. If the session is playing when you click the slider, the session will continue playing at the point you select. If the session is paused when you click the slider, the session will be positioned at the point you select and will play from that point when you next click the Play control.

Step Backward and Forward—click the left-facing triangle with bar to stop the session (if it's playing) and step backward through the session. Click the right-facing triangle with bar to stop the session (if it's playing) and step forward through the session. This control moves the video one frame at a time; to rewind or fast forward, hold the control down. The session will play from the stopping point when you next click the Play control.

A typical interaction might be:

1. Click the Observe tab.

   (Session begins playing.)

2. Click the Show/Hide sidebar to show the counselor response, intent, and focus.

Exercise for Session 1

For exercise 1, you are asked to identify the counseling response for the 16 counselor responses in the session.

The video will automatically pause after each counselor response during the session, and you will be presented with a list of counseling responses from which to choose. Select the one you feel best represents the counseling response the counselor has just given. Then compare your selection to the suggested counseling response and proceed to the next interaction.

For each exercise, the session video is completely controlled for you. You need only signal when you are ready to begin and to move on. To begin the exercise, click the Begin button to the left of the video window. Once the exercise has begun, this button will change to Next. Next is used to advance the session to the next interaction after you have identified the response and compared.

The Repeat button to the left of the video window repeats the most recent client/counselor interaction. If you choose a different tab at the top of the screen after you have started an exercise, your place will be saved for you. When you return to the exercise you can click Repeat to proceed.

To change the volume of the session, click the Volume button in the lower right corner of the screen. Click the Up Arrow to increase the volume and the Down Arrow to lower it. When you reach maximum or minimum volume, the arrow will turn gray. If an acceptable volume cannot be found, you may need to exit the CD-ROM and change the system volume of your computer. When you restart the CD-ROM, you will likely have a more acceptable range of volume control.

The video will stop after each counselor response. When the video stops, click Identify Response. The intent and focus will be shown in the appropriate spaces. Choose the counseling response that best represents what the counselor has just said from the list of 15 possible counseling responses. After you have chosen the response, click Compare to see how the identified response compares with the suggested response. To move on to the next interaction, click Next.

If you choose to save your work for the session, your identified responses will be saved. When you have completed the entire exercise, click the Reflect tab shown at the top of the screen to answer the reflection questions for this session.

A typical interaction might be:

1. Select session 1 on the Select screen.
2. Click the Exercise tab.
3. Click the Begin button.

   (Session plays.)
   (Session stops after counselor response.)

4. Click the Identify sidebar.

   (List of response types displayed.)

5. Select a response type from the list by clicking on it.

   (Selection is displayed in the student area.)

6. Click the Compare sidebar.

   (Suggested response displayed for comparison.)

7. Click Next button.

   (Session resumes play.)
   (Session stops after counselor response.)

8. Repeat beginning with step 4 until session completes.

Exercise for Session 2

For exercise 2, you are asked to identify the counseling response for the 26 counselor responses in the session.

The video will automatically pause after each counselor response during the session, and you will be presented with a list of responses from which to choose. Select the one you feel best represents the counseling response the counselor has just given. Then compare your selection to the suggested counseling response and proceed to the next interaction.

For each exercise, the session video is completely controlled for you. You need only signal when you are ready to begin and to move on. To begin the exercise, click the Begin button to the left of the video window. Once the exercise has begun, this button will change to Next. Next is used to advance the session to the next interaction after you have identified the response and compared.

The Repeat button to the left of the video window repeats the most recent client/counselor interaction. If you choose a different tab at the top of the screen after you have started an exercise, your place will be saved for you. When you return to the exercise you can click Repeat to proceed.

To change the volume of the session, click the Volume button in the lower right corner of the screen. Click the Up Arrow to increase the volume and the Down Arrow to lower it. When you reach maximum or minimum volume, the arrow will turn gray. If an acceptable volume cannot be found, you may need to exit the CD-ROM and change the system volume of your computer. When you restart the CD-ROM, you will likely have a more acceptable range of volume control.

The video will stop after each counselor response. When the video stops, click Identify Response. The intent and focus will be shown in the appropriate spaces. Choose the response that best represents what the counselor has just said from the list of 15 possible counseling responses. After you have chosen the response, click Compare to see how the identified response compares with the suggested response. To move on to the next interaction, click Next.

If you choose to save your work for the session, your identified responses will be saved. When you have completed the entire exercise, click the Reflect tab shown at the top of the screen to answer the reflection questions for this session.

A typical interaction might be:

1. Select session 2 on the Select screen.
2. Click the Exercise tab.
3. Click the Begin button.

    (Session plays.)
    (Session stops after counselor response.)

4. Click the Identify sidebar.

    (List of response types displayed.)

5. Select a response type from the list by clicking on it.

    (Selection is displayed in the student area.)

6. Click the Compare sidebar.

   (Suggested response displayed for comparison.)

7. Click Next button.

   (Session resumes play.)
   (Session stops after counselor response.)

8. Repeat beginning with step 4 until session completes.

Exercise for Session 3

For exercise 3, you are asked to identify the focus for the 23 counselor responses in the session.

The video will automatically pause after each counselor response during the session, and you will be presented with a list of focuses from which to choose. Select the one you feel best represents the focus of the counselor response just given. Then compare your selection to the suggested focus and proceed to the next interaction.

For each exercise, the session video is completely controlled for you. You need only signal when you are ready to begin and to move on. To begin the exercise, click the Begin button to the left of the video window. Once the exercise has begun, this button will change to Next. Next is used to advance the session to the next interaction after you have identified the focus and compared.

The Repeat button to the left of the video window repeats the most recent client/counselor interaction. If you choose a different tab at the top of the screen after you have started an exercise, your place will be saved for you. When you return to the exercise you can click Repeat to proceed.

To change the volume of the session, click the Volume button in the lower right corner of the screen. Click the Up Arrow to increase the volume and the Down Arrow to lower it. When you reach maximum or minimum volume, the arrow will turn gray. If an acceptable volume cannot be found, you may need to exit the CD-ROM and change the system volume of your computer. When you restart the CD-ROM, you will likely have a more acceptable range of volume control.

The video will stop after each counseling response. When the video stops, click Identify Focus. The response and intent will be shown in the appropriate spaces. Choose the focus that best represents what the counselor has just said from the list of 4 possible focuses, adding the additional focus of immediacy if appropriate. After you have chosen the focus, click Compare to see how the identified focus compares with the suggested focus. To move on to the next interaction, click Next.

If you choose to save your work for the session, your identified focuses will be saved. When you have completed the entire exercise, click the Reflect tab shown at the top of the screen to answer the reflection questions for this session.

A typical interaction might be:

1. Select session 3 on the Select screen.
2. Click the Exercise tab.

3. Click the Begin button.

   (Session plays.)
   (Session stops after counselor response.)

4. Click the Identify Focus sidebar.

   (List of focuses displayed.)

5. Select a focus from the list by clicking on it.

   (Selection is displayed in the student area.)

6. Click the Compare sidebar.

   (Suggested focus displayed for comparison.)

7. Click Next button.

   (Session resumes play.)
   (Session stops after counselor response.)

8. Repeat beginning with step 4 until session completes.

Exercise for Session 4

For exercise 4, you are asked to identify the intent of the 34 counselor responses in the session.

The video will automatically pause after each counselor response during the session, and you will be presented with a list of intents from which to choose. Select the one you feel best represents the intent of the counselor response just given. Then compare your selection to the suggested intent and proceed to the next interaction.

For each exercise, the session video is completely controlled for you. You need only signal when you are ready to begin and to move on. To begin the exercise, click the Begin button to the left of the video window. Once the exercise has begun, this button will change to Next. Next is used to advance the session to the next interaction after you have identified the focus and compared.

The Repeat button to the left of the video window repeats the most recent client/counselor interaction. If you choose a different tab at the top of the screen after you have started an exercise, your place will be saved for you. When you return to the exercise you can click Repeat to proceed.

To change the volume of the session, click the Volume button in the lower right corner of the screen. Click the Up Arrow to increase the volume and the Down Arrow to lower it. When you reach maximum or minimum volume, the arrow will turn gray. If an acceptable volume cannot be found, you may need to exit the CD-ROM and change the system volume of your computer. When you restart the CD-ROM, you will likely have a more acceptable range of volume control.

The video will stop after each counseling response. When the video stops, click Identify Intent. The response and focus will be shown in the appropriate spaces. Choose the intent that best represents what the counselor has just said from the list of 3 possible intents. After you have chosen the intent, click Compare to see how the identified intent compares with the suggested intent. To move on to the next interaction, click Next.

If you choose to save your work for the session, your identified intents will be saved. When you have completed the entire exercise, click the Reflect tab shown at the top of the screen to answer the reflection questions for this session.

A typical interaction might be:

1. Select session 4 on the Select screen.
2. Click the Exercise tab.
3. Click the Begin button.

   (Session plays.)
   (Session stops after counselor response.)

4. Click the Identify Intent sidebar.

   (List of intents displayed.)

5. Select an intent from the list by clicking on it.

   (Selection is displayed in the student area.)

6. Click the Compare sidebar.

   (Suggested intent displayed for comparison.)

7. Click Next button.

   (Session resumes play.)
   (Session stops after counselor response.)

8. Repeat beginning with step 4 until session completes.

Exercise for Session 5

For exercise 5, you are asked to identify the response, intent, and focus of the 43 counselor responses in the session.

The video will automatically pause after each counselor response during the session, and you will be presented with a list of response types, intents, and focuses from which to choose. Select the response, intent, and focus you feel best represent the counselor response the counselor has just given. Then compare your selections to the suggested selections and proceed to the next interaction.

For each exercise, the session video is completely controlled for you. You need only signal when you are ready to begin and to move on. To begin the exercise, click the Begin button to the left of the video window. Once the exercise has begun, this button will change to Next. Next is used to advance the session to the next interaction after you have identified the focus and compared.

The Repeat button to the left of the video window repeats the most recent client/counselor interaction. If you choose a different tab at the top of the screen after you have started an exercise, your place will be saved for you. When you return to the exercise you can click Repeat to proceed.

To change the volume of the session, click the Volume button in the lower right corner of the screen. Click the Up Arrow to increase the volume and the Down Arrow to lower it. When you reach maximum or minimum volume, the arrow will turn gray. If an acceptable volume cannot be found, you may need to exit the CD-ROM and change the system volume of your computer. When you restart the CD-ROM, you will likely have a more acceptable range of volume control.

The video will stop after each counseling response. When the video stops, click Identify Response, Identify Intent, or Identify Focus (identification of the response, intent, and focus may be done in any order). The corresponding selection list will be displayed. Choose the response, intent, or focus that best represents what the counselor has just said from the list. After you have identified the response, intent, and focus, click Compare to see how your three selections compare with the suggested selections. To move on to the next interaction, click Next.

If you choose to save your work for the session, your identified responses, intents, and focuses will be saved. When you have completed the entire exercise, click the Reflect tab shown at the top of the screen to answer the reflection questions for this session.

A typical interaction might be:

1. Select session 5 on the Select screen.
2. Click the Exercise tab.
3. Click the Begin button.

    (Session plays.)
    (Session stops after counselor response.)

4. Click the Identify Response sidebar.

    (List of response types displayed.)

5. Select a response type from the list by clicking on it.

    (Selection is displayed in the student area.)

6. Click the Identify Intent sidebar.

    (List of intents displayed.)

7. Select an intent from the list by clicking on it.

    (Selection is displayed in the student area.)

8. Click the Identify Focus sidebar.

    (List of focuses displayed.)

9. Select a focus from the list by clicking on it.

    (Selection is displayed in the student area.)

10. Click the Compare sidebar.

    (Suggested response type, intent, and focus displayed for comparison.)

11. Click Next button.

(Session resumes play.)
(Session stops after counselor response.)

12. Repeat beginning with step 4 until session completes.

Exercise for Session 6

For exercise 6, you are asked to type in a student-created verbatim response that exemplifies the given response, intent, and focus at three points during the session when the counselor responds. Your verbatim response should be in reaction to what the client has just said. However, the client response may not follow your verbatim response.

The video will automatically pause just prior to counselor responses at 6.9, 6.14, and 6.19, and the given counseling response, intent, and focus will be displayed. Type in a student-created verbatim response and compare that response to the counselor's actual response. After comparing, continue the session with the next interaction.

For each exercise, the session video is completely controlled for you. You need only signal when you are ready to begin and to move on. To begin the exercise, click the Begin button to the left of the video window. Once the exercise has begun, this button will change to Next. Next is used to advance the session to the next designated interaction after you have given your verbatim response and compared.

The Repeat button to the left of the video window repeats the most recent client statement or counselor response. If you choose a different tab at the top of the screen after you have started an exercise, your place will be saved for you. When you return to the exercise you can click Repeat to proceed.

To change the volume of the session, click the Volume button in the lower right corner of the screen. Click the Up Arrow to increase the volume and the Down Arrow to lower it. When you reach maximum or minimum volume, the arrow will turn gray. If an acceptable volume cannot be found, you may need to exit the CD-ROM and change the system volume of your computer. When you restart the CD-ROM, you will likely have a more acceptable range of volume control.

The video will stop just prior to the three designated counselor responses. When the video stops, the identified response, intent, and focus will be shown in the appropriate spaces. Click Create Response, then click inside the student verbatim response area and begin typing your response. (If you fill the area with your response, use the scroll bar on the right to review your entire response.) After you have completed your response, click Compare to see how the verbatim response compares with the counselor's actual response. To move on to the next interaction, click Next.

If you choose to save your work for the session, your verbatim responses will be saved. When you have completed the entire exercise, click the Reflect tab shown at the top of the screen to answer the reflection questions for this session.

A typical interaction might be:

1. Select session 6 on the Select screen.
2. Click the Exercise tab.
3. Click the Begin button.

(Session plays.)

(Session stops just prior to counselor response.)
(Response type, intent, and focus displayed.)

4. Click the Create Response sidebar.
5. Click in the student verbatim response area and type in a response.
6. Click the Compare sidebar.

    (Counselor's actual response displayed for comparison.)
    (Session resumes play and stops at the end of the counselor's actual response.)

7. Click the Next button.

    (Session resumes play.)
    (Session stops just prior to counselor response.)
    (Response type, intent, and focus displayed.)

8. Repeat beginning with step 4 until session completes.

Exercise for Session 7

For exercise 7, you are asked to identify the counseling response, intent, and focus you feel are most appropriate at five points during the session when the counselor responds. You are also asked to type in a student-created verbatim response that exemplifies your identified response, intent, and focus. Your verbatim response should be in reaction to what the client has just said. However, the client response may not follow your verbatim response.

The video will automatically pause just prior to counselor responses at 7.4, 7.9, 7.13, 7.17, and 7.19, and you will be presented with a list of responses, intents, and focuses from which to choose. Identify the response, intent, and focus you feel would be most appropriate at this point in the session and type a student-created verbatim response that exemplifies your identified response, intent, and focus. Then compare your selections to the suggested selections and your verbatim response to the counselor's actual response. After comparing, continue the session with the next interaction.

For each exercise, the session video is completely controlled for you. You need only signal when you are ready to begin and to move on. To begin the exercise, click the Begin button to the left of the video window. Once the exercise has begun, this button will change to Next. Next is used to advance the session to the next designated interaction after you have made your selections, given your verbatim response, and compared.

The Repeat button to the left of the video window repeats the most recent client statement or counselor response. If you choose a different tab at the top of the screen after you have started an exercise, your place will be saved for you. When you return to the exercise you can click Repeat to proceed.

To change the volume of the session, click the Volume button in the lower right corner of the screen. Click the Up Arrow to increase the volume and the Down Arrow to lower it. When you reach maximum or minimum volume, the arrow will turn gray. If an acceptable volume cannot be found, you may need to exit the CD-ROM and change the system volume of your computer. When you restart the CD-ROM, you will likely have a more acceptable range of volume control.

The video will stop just prior to the five designated counselor responses. When the video stops, click Identify Response, Identify Intent, or Identify Focus (identification of the response, intent, and focus may be done in any order). The corresponding selection list will be displayed. Choose the response, intent, or focus that you feel is most appropriate from the list. After you have identified the response, intent, and focus, click Create Response. Then click inside the student verbatim response area and begin typing your response. (If you fill the area with your response, use the scroll bar on the right to review your entire response.) After you have completed your response, click Compare to see how your three selections compare with the suggested selections and how your verbatim response compares with the counselor's actual response. To move on to the next interaction, click Next.

If you choose to save your work for the session, your selected responses, intents, and focuses along with your verbatim responses will be saved. When you have completed the entire exercise, click the Reflect tab shown at the top of the screen to answer the reflection questions for this session.

A typical interaction might be:

1. Select session 7 on the Select screen.
2. Click the Exercise tab.
3. Click the Begin button.

   (Session plays.)
   (Session stops just prior to counselor response.)

4. Click the Identify Response sidebar.

   (List of response types displayed.)

5. Select a response type from the list by clicking on it.

   (Selection is displayed in the student area.)

6. Click the Identify Intent sidebar.

   (List of intents displayed.)

7. Select an intent from the list by clicking on it.

   (Selection is displayed in the student area.)

8. Click the Identify Focus sidebar.

   (List of focuses displayed.)

9. Select a focus from the list by clicking on it.

   (Selection is displayed in the student area.)

10. Click the Create Response sidebar.
11. Click in the student verbatim response area and type in a response.
12. Click the Compare sidebar.

    (Suggested response type, intent, and focus displayed for comparison.)
    (Counselor's actual response displayed for comparison.)
    (Session resumes play and stops at the end of the counselor's actual response.)

13. Click Next button.

(Session stops just prior to counselor response.)

14. Repeat beginning with step 4 until session completes.

Reflecting on a Session

Each session has 2 to 5 questions for you to reflect on and optionally answer. You may answer the reflection questions at any time, although some of the reflection questions assume you have completed the exercise associated with the session. You can view the reflection questions at any time by clicking the Reflect tab. You can return there repeatedly to add to or change your answers prior to saving your work.

To view the first reflection question, click Answer Next. To type in an answer for this question, click in the answer area on the right and begin typing. To answer the next question, click Answer Next again. When you reach the last question for the session, clicking Answer Next will display the first question along with your answer if you have given one. Answer Previous allows you to go back to the previous question in the list.

If you choose to save your work for the session, your answers to the reflection questions will be saved.

A typical interaction might be:

1. Click the Reflect tab.
2. Click the Next Question sidebar.

(Reflection question #1 is displayed.)

3. Click in the student answer area and type in your answer.
4. Click the Next Question sidebar.

(Next reflection question is displayed.)

5. Repeat beginning with step 3 until all questions are answered.

Filing a Session

Select the File tab to save the work you have done on the current session. The data that are saved include your work on the exercises (identification of response, intent, and/or focus, and keyboarded verbatim responses, if any) along with your answers to the reflection questions. You can save partial work to be continued momentarily, partial work to be completed at another time, or completed work to be printed for personal reference or submission as coursework.

If you save your work by clicking Save Work, it will be written to a floppy disk or your computer's hard drive. You can save at any time and still continue working on the current session. Your work will not be cleared from the CD-ROM exercise and reflection areas until you choose another session or quit the CD-ROM. At that time, if you have work pending that has not been saved, you will be asked to either save or not save the work before continuing.

When you click Do Not Save, your work is cleared from the CD-ROM exercise and reflection areas. If you think you might want to complete or reference the work you are doing again, you should save the work.

When you save your work, you are asked where the information should be written. You must specify the desired hard drive or floppy disk and the desired folder or directory. You will use a standard PC or Mac file location dialog box for this specification. A suggested file name will be provided as a default. The easiest and safest course is to accept the default file name. If you want to change the file name, review the important file-naming guidelines at the end of this help information.

When you save your work, two files are written to disk. For example, when you save the work for session 4, the file save dialog box will display the default name of "bcr4". If you accept this default, your two files for session 4 will be named:

bcr4.TXT
bcr4.BCR

and will be placed in the folder or directory on the disk you specified. If you are using a PC, the configuration of your Windows system may cause the "TXT" extension to be hidden in the folder view. In this case, your two files for session 4 will be named:

bcr4
bcr4.BCR

The "TXT" or text file can be loaded into a word processing program for desired formatting and printing. For example, you might want to add your name and the date to the top of the pages. Feel free to edit and save this file as you wish. For best results, always print the text file from a word processing program. For tips on how to load the text file into a word processing program, see the printing guidelines at the end of this help information.

The "BCR" file should never be edited or renamed. This file contains your exercise and reflection work in a form suitable for reloading into the CD-ROM using Get Saved Work on the Select screen. You may delete this file when you no longer want to save the work it contains for the session.

If problems are encountered during the file save operation, you will be informed in the message area in the lower portion of the screen. Normally, you will see the message "Your work has been successfully saved."

Printing Guidelines

The text file is a simple text file that can be opened by or "imported" into most word processing programs. If your program has an open or import option for text files, choose it. If the dialog asks for a file type, specify "ASCII Text" or just "Text." Then locate the desired text file on your floppy disk or hard drive. Most of the time, your work should import without difficulties. You can then edit your file and print it. It is not necessary to save the imported file after you have printed it, although you may do so if you wish.

If your work does not import successfully (appears to be empty or unrecognizable), you can try another approach. Locate your "TXT" file on your floppy disk or hard drive. Double click the file to open it with your computer's default editor (usually Notepad on a PC and SimpleText on a Mac). From the Edit menu at the top of the screen, choose Select All, then from the same menu choose Copy. Open a new document in your word processing program and choose Paste from the Edit menu. All your work should appear in the new document, ready for editing and printing. If neither of these approaches is successful, seek assistance.

File-Naming Guidelines

Provide a file name only. The CD-ROM will add the extensions ".TXT" and ".BCR" to the name you provide. For example, if you choose the name "session6partial", the CD-ROM will name the two files "session6partial.TXT" and "session6partial.BCR". If you are using a PC, the configuration of your Windows system may cause the "TXT" extension to be hidden in the folder view.

A typical interaction might be:

1. Click the File tab.
2. Click the Save Work sidebar to save the work on the current session.
3. Specify a hard disk or floppy disk location along with a directory or folder; use the default file name suggested for the files.
4. Load the text file (default bcr#.TXT) into a word processing program for formatting and printing.

Quitting the CD-ROM

Select the Quit tab to exit the *Basic Counseling Responses* CD-ROM. Once the Quit screen is displayed, you can actually exit by clicking Exit, or you can return to *Basic Counseling Responses* by clicking any of the tabs at the top of the screen. Click Credits to learn more about the making of the *Basic Counseling Responses* CD-ROM.

If you have worked on an exercise or have answered some reflection questions for a session, you will not be able to exit the CD-ROM until you save or choose not to save your work.

A typical interaction might be:
1. Click the Quit tab.
2. Click the Exit sidebar to exit the *Basic Counseling Responses* CD-ROM.

Troubleshooting Guide

If you don't find the answer to your question in this section, please contact Technical Support at Brooks/Cole•Wadsworth Publishing Company:

Phone: 1-800-423-0563
Fax: 1-606-647-5045
Email: Support@kdc.com

Symptom (not enough memory):
After double-clicking on BasicCR.exe, the program displays a message indicating there is not enough memory to run the program.

Solution: BasicCR requires a mimimum amount of memory to run efficiently. You may be able to run the program in less than the recommended amount, however, you may encounter some performance problems like stuttering video and the video's audio track becoming out of sync with the picture.

Symptom (no video display):
After starting up BasicCR.exe by double-clicking, there is no video displayed when selecting a session to watch or you get a message that QuickTime is not installed.

Solution: You have not installed Apple's QuickTime 3.0 video drivers. This CD uses video that was compressed using Apple Computer's QuickTime video technology. You must have the QuickTime video drivers installed on your PC before *Basic Counseling Responses* will play the video. The QuickTime drivers are provided on this CD if you do not already have them.
You need to run the setup.exe program located in the folder QT3/disks/.
Locate the setup program (setup.exe) and double-click on the icon.
This setup program will install Apple's new version of QuickTime 3.0 for Windows95 and the older version of QuickTime 2.1.2 for Windows.
Basic Counseling Responses needs QuickTime 2.1.2 for Windows as well as QuickTime 3.0 for Windows.
After installation, reboot your PC and you should be able to run the video.

Symptom (no sound):
There is no sound playing when *Basic Counseling Responses* runs.

Solution: Check to be sure that you have a "Sound Blaster 16 bit" compatible sound card installed and speakers, or headphones, connected to your PC. *Basic Counseling Responses* requires this equipment in order to play its audio.
Make sure the volume of your sound card is set to an audible range.
There is volume control inside BCR, but it is better to start with the system volume set in the upper 30% range.

Symptom (poor color quality):
The color isn't very good in the program.

Solution: Set your display or monitor to 16-bit ("thousands") color. You will find the controls for your color settings in the Control Panels section under "Display."

Symptom (poor video quality):
Video performance is sluggish or the audio is out of sync with the picture.

Solution: There are a number of things that can cause this problem.

You may not have enough memory installed in your computer. We recommend at least 24 MB of RAM.

Your computer may not be fast enough. We recommend at least a 66 MHz Pentium.

Your CD-ROM drive may be too slow. We recommend at least a 2x CD-ROM drive.

The computer's display card that runs your monitor may not have enough speed to support video playback. You may want to set the color depth to "256." The "thousands of colors" setting in your display demands more performance from your computer. The color will not be as good when set at "256," but the video will run better.

You may have other programs open while you are running *Basic Counseling Responses.* You can improve performance by closing all other programs and windows.

The out-of-sync problem can appear after viewing multiple sessions in a row. If this occurs, exit *Basic Counseling Responses* and restart. If the problem does not go away, then exit *Basic Counseling Responses,* reboot your computer, and restart the program.

Note: See the Troubleshooting file on the CD-ROM for the latest information.

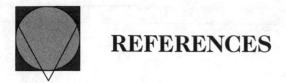

REFERENCES

Belkin, G. S. (1984). *Introduction to counseling.* Dubuque, IA: Brown.

Corey, G., Corey, M. S., & Callahan, P. (1998). *Issues and ethics in the helping professions* (5th ed.). Pacific Grove, CA: Brooks/Cole.

Egan, G. (1994). *The skilled helper* (5th ed.). Pacific Grove, CA: Brooks/Cole.

Egan, G. (1986). *The skilled helper* (3rd ed.). Pacific Grove, CA: Brooks/Cole.

Egan, G. (1985). *Exercises in helping skills* (3rd ed.). Pacific Grove, CA: Brooks/Cole.

Ivey, A. E. (1994). *Intentional interviewing and counseling: Facilitating client development* (3rd ed.). Pacific Grove, CA: Brooks/Cole.

Kleinke, C. L. (1994). *Common principles of psychotherapy.* Pacific Grove, CA: Brooks/Cole.

Kottler, J. A., & Brown, R. W. (1996). *Introduction to therapeutic counseling* (3rd ed.). Pacific Grove, CA: Brooks/Cole.

Lauver, P., & Harvey, D. R. (1997). *The practical counselor: Elements of effective counseling.* Pacific Grove, CA: Brooks/Cole.

Meier, S. T., & Davis, S. R. (1997). *The elements of counseling* (3rd ed.). Pacific Grove, CA: Brooks/Cole.

Moursund, J. (1993). *The process of counseling and therapy.* Pacific Grove, CA: Brooks/Cole.

Okun, B. F. (1997). *Effective helping: Interviewing and counseling techniques* (5th ed.). Pacific Grove, CA: Brooks/Cole.

Sue, D. W., Ivey, A. E., & Pedersen, P. B. (1996). *A theory of multicultural counseling and therapy.* Pacific Grove, CA: Brooks/Cole.

INDEX

TO THE OWNER OF THIS PACKAGE

We are very interested in learning more about *how* you are using the components of *Basic Counseling Responses* (worktext, videocassette, and CD-ROM). Please take a moment to fill out this MULTIMEDIA SURVEY:

Name: _____ School: _____

Course: _____ E-mail: _____

Instructor: _____

1. Are you using all the components of this package? If not, which are you using and why? Which have you not used yet, and why?

2. Please share your impressions of this package? How is it helping you to learn? How could it be even better?

3. Do you have easy access to a VCR?   ○ Yes   ○ No
   If yes, is it your own VCR or the property of the school?

4. Do you have easy access to a computer?   ○ Yes   ○ No
   If yes, is it your own computer or the property of the school?

5. Do you have access to computer labs for learning concepts in specific coursework?   ○ Yes   ○ No
   If yes, which courses?

   Instructor(s):
6. How many computer labs are available?   ○ 0 ○ 1 ○ 2 ○ 3 ○ 4 ○ 5 ○ Greater than 5 How many? _____

7. How many computers, on average, are in each of these labs?
   ○ < 10   ○ 10–20   ○ 21–30   ○ 31–50   ○ 51–100   ○ >100

8. Are any of these labs for the exclusive use of your program's department? ○ Yes ○ No
   If yes, how many computers do you have exclusive department rights to? _____
   If no, what other departments do you share with?
   ○ Sociology   ○ Psychology   ○ Education   ○ Other: _____

9. How are you currently using your computer lab(s)? (check as many as apply)
   ○ For free time, to complete assignments/homework
   ○ Used during designated computer lab time, access to technology products/tools to complete specific assignments
   ○ Primary location where your classes meet
   ○ You don't use the computer lab(s)
   ○ Other: _____

10. What operating system do you use personally?
    ○ Win 95   ○ Win 3.1   ○ Win NT   ○ Macintosh   ○ Unix   ○ OS2   ○ Mix of Win and Mac

11. What is the current dominant operating system in your computer lab(s)?
    ○ Win 95   ○ Win 3.1   ○ Win NT   ○ Macintosh   ○ Unix   ○ OS2   ○ Mix of Win and Mac

12. What operating system do think will be dominant in two years?
    ○ Win 98   ○ Win 95   ○ Win 3.1   ○ Win NT   ○ Macintosh   ○ Unix   ○ OS2

13. When do you think technology will be used by a majority of your instructors as part of their course(s)?
    ○ Never   ○ 1998   ○ 1999   ○ 2000   ○ 2001   ○ 2002   ○ > 2002   ○ A majority already is

14. Do you currently use the Web in your course(s)?   ○ Yes   ○ No   If yes, how are you using the Web?
    ○ To obtain raw data for various assignments and labs
    ○ To find information on topics discussed in class or discovered in this package
    ○ To access information from a textbook publisher's Web server
    ○ To access information from a software publisher's Web server
    ○ For a distance/distributed learning environment where some students are off-site/not in your classroom
    ○ Other: _____

Any other comments?

Optional:

Your name: _____ Date: _____

May Brooks/Cole•Wadsworth quote you, either in promotion for *Basic Counseling Responses* or in future publishing ventures?

Yes: _____ No: _____

Sincerely,

Hutch Haney
Jacqueline Leibsohn